CAMBRIDGE
Lower Secondary
Global Perspectives

Rob Bircher, Mike Gould, Mark Pedroz and Ed Walsh

Series Editor: Mark Pedroz

Stage 7: Student's Book

Published by Collins

An imprint of HarperCollins*Publishers*

The News Building, 1 London Bridge Street, London, SE1 9GF, UK

HarperCollins*Publishers*
Macken House, 39/40 Mayor Street Upper, Dublin 1,
D01 C9W8, Ireland

Browse the complete Collins catalogue at
www.collins.co.uk

© HarperCollinsPublishers Limited 2023

10 9 8 7 6 5 4 3 2 1

ISBN 978-0-00-854934-3

British Library Cataloguing-in-Publication Data

A catalogue record for this publication is available from the British Library.

Series editor: Mark Pedroz
Authors: Rob Bircher, Mike Gould, Mark Pedroz and Ed Walsh
Publisher: Elaine Higgleton
Product manager: Catherine Martin
Project manager and development editor: Caroline Low
Copy editor: Susan Ross, Ross Economics and Editorial Services Ltd
Proofreader: Claire Throp
Cover designer: Gordon McGilp
Cover image: Ann Paganuzzi
Internal designer: Ken Vail Graphic Design
Typesetter: David Jimenez
Production controller: Lyndsey Rogers
Printed and bound by Grafica Veneta S.p.A.

MIX
Paper | Supporting responsible forestry
FSC™ C007454

Acknowledgements

We are grateful to the following teachers for providing feedback on the Stage 7 Student's Book in development:

Ms Deepa Maurya, Science, Biology and Global Perspectives teacher, Bombay Cambridge International School, Andheri (E), India; Paula Gemelur and Maria Laura Calderon, Escuela Argentina Modelo, Buenos Aires, Argentina; Shaheen Mohamed, Westcoast International Secondary School, Cascavelle, Mauritius; Mr Akash Raut, Principal of Firststeps IB World School, Chandigarh, India.

Contents

Introduction: How to use this book

The Collins Stage 7 Student's Book offers an introduction to Cambridge Global Perspectives™ at Lower Secondary level, with rich international texts, data and case studies to stimulate your thinking about contemporary global topics.

The book is organised into seven chapters. Each chapter explores different issues and perspectives that are relevant to one of the syllabus topics. In Stage 7, the topics you will explore are 'Change in culture and communities', 'Education for all', 'Health and wellbeing', 'Globalisation', 'Values and beliefs', 'Employment' and 'Environment, pollution and conservation'.

Chapter 1 introduces the fundamentals of *collaboration*, *communication* and *reflection*, skills which will support you in all the work you do in later chapters to develop the six strands of Global Perspectives.

In Chapter 2, you will learn about carrying out *research*, locating information in a range of sources and how to begin *evaluating* those sources and the perspectives they present.

Chapter 3 will help you to *analyse* the different ways in which data can be presented. You will then *evaluate* how data and other forms of evidence can be used to support arguments, make predictions and help you choose from a range of given solutions.

In Chapter 4, you will develop these skills further by beginning to *analyse* the causes and consequences of an issue. You will *reflect* on how your personal viewpoint on an issue may have developed or changed through the process of *evaluating* different perspectives.

Chapter 5 will develop your *communication* and *collaboration* skills, with an emphasis on learning about teamwork and boosting your confidence in presenting to others.

In Chapter 6, you will work *collaboratively* as a group to *find solutions*, considering how teamwork can be organised effectively and improved.

Chapters 2–6 each build to a final task that gives you the opportunity to draw together and apply your learning, as you investigate an issue from the chapter in more depth.

Finally, Chapter 7 allows you and your teachers to assess your progress, as you draw together your understanding from earlier chapters to undertake a mini project. You will work first in a team to research and take action on a local issue and then on your own to produce a reflective report.

We hope our resources will support you to build skills that you can use in all the subjects you study at Lower Secondary. We hope, too, that the sources you encounter in the book will inspire you to investigate other global issues – the issues that are most important to you, your school, your culture, your local environment and the nation(s) to which you belong.

Mark Pedroz, Series Editor

Key features of the Student's Book

The **opening page** of each chapter summarises the skills, topic and issues to be explored, as well as the final task.

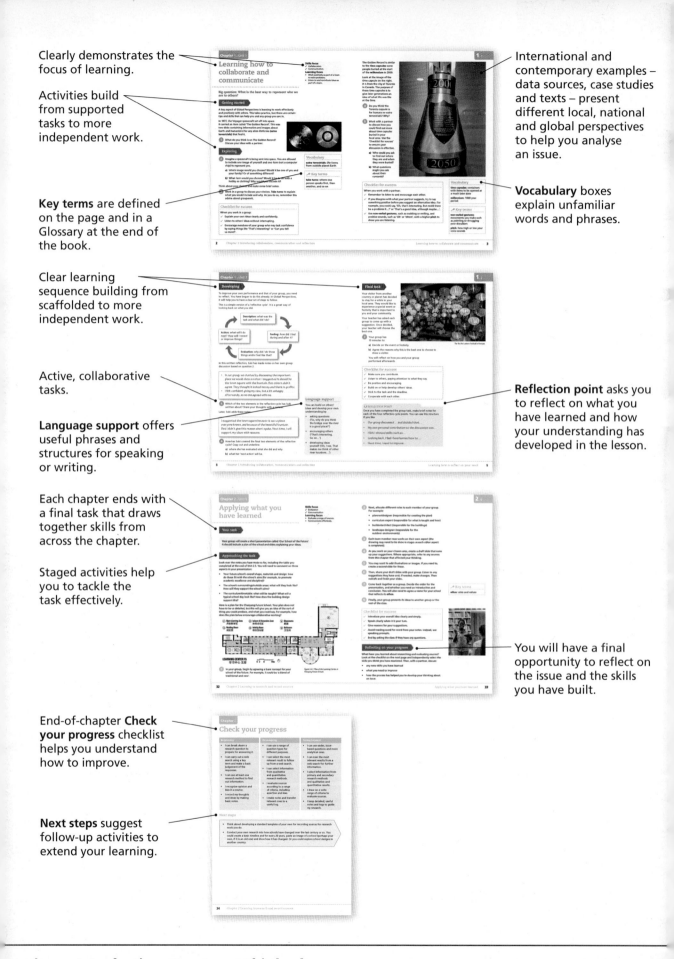

Clearly demonstrates the focus of learning.

Activities build from supported tasks to more independent work.

Key terms are defined on the page and in a Glossary at the end of the book.

Clear learning sequence building from scaffolded to more independent work.

Active, collaborative tasks.

Language support offers useful phrases and structures for speaking or writing.

Each chapter ends with a final task that draws together skills from across the chapter.

Staged activities help you to tackle the task effectively.

End-of-chapter **Check your progress** checklist helps you understand how to improve.

Next steps suggest follow-up activities to extend your learning.

International and contemporary examples – data sources, case studies and texts – present different local, national and global perspectives to help you analyse an issue.

Vocabulary boxes explain unfamiliar words and phrases.

Reflection point asks you to reflect on what you have learned and how your understanding has developed in the lesson.

You will have a final opportunity to reflect on the issue and the skills you have built.

Introducing collaboration, communication and reflection

1

Representing ourselves to others

We all care about how we appear to others. But have you ever thought about how later generations, perhaps space travellers of the future, might view us? This unit will explore how we see ourselves, our community and our school, by looking at time capsules and how they are used.

In this chapter, you will be exploring the topic of 'Changing cultures and communities', thinking about the following issues:

- **What is the best way to represent who we are to others?**

- **What makes you proud about yourself, your home and your culture?**

You will be developing a range of collaborative, communicative and reflective skills:

1.1 Learning how to collaborate and communicate

1.2 Learning how to reflect on your work.

Your final task will be to work with your group to agree a community event or festivity to show to a visitor, and to present your findings to your teacher.

Learning how to collaborate and communicate

Skills focus
✓ Collaboration
✓ Communication
Learning focus
• Work positively as part of a team to solve problems.
• Listen to and contribute ideas as part of a team.

Big question: What is the best way to represent who we are to others?

Getting started

A key aspect of Global Perspectives is learning to work effectively and positively with others. This takes practice, but there are certain tips and skills that can help you and any group you are in.

In 1977, the Voyager spacecraft set off into space. It carried an item called 'The Golden Record'. This was two disks containing information and images about Earth and humankind for any alien lifeforms (**extra terrestrials**) that find it.

1   What do you think is on The Golden Record? Discuss your ideas with a partner.

Exploring

2   Imagine a spacecraft is being sent into space. You are allowed to include one image of yourself and one item (not a computer chip) to represent you.

a) Which image would you choose? Would it be one of you and your family? Or of something different?

b) What item would you choose? Would it be to do with a hobby or clothing? Why would you include it?

Think about your choices and make some brief notes.

3   Work in a group to discuss your choices. **Take turns** to explain what you would include and why. As you do so, remember this advice about groupwork.

Vocabulary

extra terrestrials: life forms from outside planet Earth

Key terms

take turns: where one person speaks first, then another, and so on

Checklist for success

When you work in a group:

✔ Explain your own ideas clearly and confidently.

✔ Listen to others' ideas without interrupting.

✔ Encourage members of your group who may lack confidence by saying things like 'That's interesting!' or 'Can you tell us more?'.

The Golden Record is similar to the **time capsules** some people buried at the start of the **millennium** in 2000.

Look at the image of the time capsule on the right. It is from the city of Toronto in Canada. The purpose of these time capsules is to give later generations an idea of what life was like at the time.

4 Do you think the Toronto capsule is for humans or extra terrestrials? Why?

5 Work with a partner to discuss how you could find out more about time capsules buried in your local area. Use the 'Checklist for success' to ensure your discussion is effective.

   a) Who could you ask to find out where they are and when they were buried?

   b) What questions might you ask about their contents?

Checklist for success

When you work with a partner:

✔ Remember to listen to and encourage each other.

✔ If you disagree with what your partner suggests, try to say something positive before you suggest an alternative idea. For example, you could say, 'Oh, that's interesting. But could there be a problem if...?' or 'That's a good idea, although maybe...'.

✔ Use **non-verbal gestures**, such as nodding or smiling, and positive sounds, such as 'Oh' or 'Mmm', with a higher **pitch** to show you are listening.

Vocabulary

time capsules: containers with items to be opened at a much later date

millennium: 1000-year period

🔑 Key terms

non-verbal gestures: movements you make such as pointing or shrugging your shoulders

pitch: how high or low your voice sounds

Working with a partner is a great way to discuss and develop your ideas. At the same time, you can also practise many of the speaking and listening skills that you use in groupwork.

Developing

Now, think about your school and the school community. How could a time capsule represent you, other students and the school as a whole? To help you think about this, look at these items placed in a capsule by one school in one country.

6 **a)** First, work on your own and make notes about the time capsule.

- What are the items in it?

- Is there anything you do not recognise or understand?

- What do the items reveal about the school? How can you tell?

b) Share your ideas with your group. As before, listen carefully – but remember to take part! Make sure someone in your group notes down everyone's ideas.

7 Read this short extract from one group's discussion and then answer the questions below.

Rava:	Well, it's clear this is a rich, posh school. They have a special uniform.
Lee:	Err. Well… I guess you could say that. But just because they have a…
Rava (interrupting):	Of course, they're posh! Don't be stupid, Lee!
Oscar:	Go on, Lee. What were you going to say?

a) Who gave their point confidently?

b) Who had a different view, but expressed it gently?

c) Who encouraged others to speak?

d) Who did not let someone finish and was rude to them?

Final task

Stay in the same group. It is now your turn to decide what could go into a time capsule to be buried in your school grounds and opened in 100 years' time. The capsule should represent your school and the school community.

8 Discuss and agree the following:

a) The six items you will place in the time capsule. The six items can include printed photos. (You are not allowed a computer chip, as technology may not be able to read the chip in 100 years' time.) For each item, you can add a very simple label or caption, for example 'a typical school meal'.

b) Where the time capsule will be buried (in or near the school?).

c) How well the time capsule represents your school and the community to others.

You must also keep your own record of what was agreed and why. You could do this using a simple table like the one below.

Item	Label	Reason
Printed photo of school lunch	A typical school lunch, e.g. tofu and noodles	To show what we ate and how vegetarian food was now more popular than meat.

Checklist for success

✔ Take turns to speak and do not interrupt.

✔ Present your own ideas confidently, supporting them with reasons.

✔ Listen carefully to others.

✔ Build on others' ideas, where appropriate.

✔ Encourage others, especially those who are shy or lack confidence.

❷ REFLECTION POINT

Once your discussion is complete, make your own notes about how well you worked as a team. Which collaboration and communication techniques did you find worked? For example, how did you support the other members of your group? Did you contribute useful ideas and offer solutions to problems? Were you open to others' ideas?

Learning how to reflect on your work

Big question: What makes you proud about yourself, your home and your culture?

Getting started

1 Each of the four images below show things people are proud about.

   a) What do you think these things or achievements are?

   b) Which of them are things you are also proud of?

   c) If you could add an image of yourself to show what you are proud of, what would it show?

The images show that you can be proud of many different things. Sometimes, these may be things you do not normally think about. However, you can practise thinking about things you have done so as to judge your own strengths and weaknesses. This is **reflection**.

Exploring

In Unit 1.1, you explored some teamwork skills. Most of these were about speaking up for yourself and listening and responding to others. There are some more key group-work skills you need to know, for example:

 **Key terms**

reflection: thinking carefully about what you or others have done, in a way which helps you make progress

- 'getting on' with each other (being friendly and generally cooperative)
- being able to stay focused on the task
- everyone in the group doing what they agreed to do
- meeting **deadlines** that have been set.

> 🔑 **Key terms**
>
> **deadline**: a set time or date by which you must complete a task

2 Think of any group or team you have been part of recently, either in school or outside of it (such as a sports team or music group).

   a) On a scale of 1 (low) to 5 (high), how well did your group do in each of the four areas described above?

   b) Where there were problems, can you think of how these could have been solved?

Effective teamwork needs practice, like any other skill. It also needs time to reflect on what went well and what did not.

3 Now that you have thought a bit about good teamwork, try this task.

> A visitor from another country (or planet!) is coming to your local area. Your group has been given the task of meeting them and showing them around. You and your group have just 20 minutes for the task.

Your group must decide on:

   a) one place that you and local people are proud about, for example, a public building or outside space

   b) one dish that showcases your local food or crops

   c) one person that you are proud of, and you think the visitor should meet – this can be an ordinary person or someone well-known.

Spend at least 5 minutes working on your own to come up with ideas, noting down any reasons for your choices. Be ready to talk about them with your group.

4 Now spend 10–15 minutes in your group, sharing ideas.

   a) Use any skills you learned about in Unit 1.1 on how to perform well in a group.

   b) Think about how good teams work together. Remember the advice given above (for example, staying focused on the task).

   c) Consider how you can listen well, by paying attention to what people say and how others respond.

Developing

To improve your own performance and that of your group, you need to reflect. You have begun to do this already. In Global Perspectives, it will help you to have a clear set of steps to follow.

This is a simple version of a 'reflective cycle'. It is a great way of looking back on what you did.

Description: *what* was the task and what *did I do*?

Feeling: *how* did I *feel* during and after it?

Action: *what* will I do *next*? How will I repeat or improve things?

Evaluation: *why did I do* those things and/or feel like that?

In this written reflection, Suki has made notes on her own group discussion based on question 2.

> • In our group, we started by discussing the important place we would show a visitor. I suggested it should be the town square with the fountain. But others didn't agree. They thought it looked messy and there is graffiti.
> • I felt confident giving my view, but a bit unhappy afterwards, as no one agreed with me.

5 Which of the two elements in the reflective cycle has Suki written about? Share your thoughts with a partner.

Later, Suki adds these notes:

> I suggested the town square because it was a place everyone knows, and because of the beautiful fountain. But I didn't give this reason when I spoke. Next time, I will support my ideas with reasons.

6 How has Suki covered the final two elements of the reflective cycle? Copy out and underline:

   a) where she has evaluated what she did and why

   b) what her 'next action' will be.

Language support

You can build on others' ideas and develop your own understanding by:

• asking questions ('So, why do you think the bridge over the river is a good place?')

• encouraging others ('That's interesting. Go on…')

• developing ideas yourself ('Ah, I see. That makes me think of other river locations…').

Final task

Your visitor from another country or planet has decided to stay for a while in your local area. They would like to experience a special event or festivity that is important to you and your community.

Your teacher has asked each group to come up with a suggestion. Once decided, your teacher will choose the best one.

7 Your group has 10 minutes to:

a) Decide on the event or festivity.

b) Agree the reasons why this is the best one to choose to show a visitor.

You will reflect on how you and your group performed afterwards.

The Hoi An Lantern Festival in Vietnam.

Checklist for success

✔ Make sure you contribute.

✔ Listen to others, paying attention to what they say.

✔ Be positive and encouraging.

✔ Build on or help develop others' ideas.

✔ Stick to the task and the deadline.

✔ Cooperate with each other.

❓ REFLECTION POINT

Once you have completed the group task, make brief notes for each of the four reflective cycle points. You can use this structure if you like.

• Our group discussed… and decided that…

• My own personal contribution to the discussion was…

• I felt I showed skills such as…

• Looking back, I feel I have learned how to…

• Next time, I need to improve…

Check your progress

Beginning	Developing	Going beyond
• I understand what I need to do to work well in a team. • I understand how a good team works together. • I can comment on some aspects of how I did in a task. • I can comment on some aspects of how our team did.	• I contribute to group discussions and sometimes listen well. • I am usually positive and stick to the task our group has been set. • I can identify some things I do well, and some things I don't do well. • I can identify some things the group does well, and some things it doesn't do well.	• I participate fully in discussions and listen carefully. • I encourage others to speak and help the group solve problems. • I can comment clearly on how I contributed and how I felt. • I can evaluate some aspects of my performance and set targets for the future.

Next steps

Find out more about The Golden Record and what was included in it for the Voyager space mission in 1977. You could also research other time capsules such as the Paris Opera Vault (1907) and the Crypt of Civilisation (1936).

Practise your reflection skills in other subjects or when you take part in events, such as a music or sports performance. You could write down a simple statement for each of the four parts of the reflective cycle:

• What I did was…

• I felt…

• I learned…

• Next time, I will…

Learning to research and record sources

Schools of the future

2

Education is a major part of your life right now. But have you ever stopped to think about the school buildings around you and the subjects you learn at school? How might schools look in the future – and what subjects might be taught?

In this chapter, you will be exploring the topic of 'Education for all', thinking about the following issues:

- **What is a 'happiness curriculum' and should every school have one?**

- **What would be a good design for a future school?**

- **What are different people's views of what a school of the future should look like?**

- **Should schools get rid of traditional subjects?**

- **Should students themselves be the ones who decide what they learn?**

You will be developing a range of research and evaluation skills:

2.1 Constructing relevant research questions on a topic

2.2 Identifying relevant sources and information

2.3 Conducting research

2.4 Evaluating sources

2.5 Recording your findings

2.6 Applying what you have learned.

Your final task will be to evaluate the sources and research you have done, and to create a group presentation called 'Our school of the future'.

Constructing relevant research questions on a topic

Skills focus
✓ Research
Learning focus
• Explore different types of question and how they can guide your research.
• Choose the best questions for the research you want to do.

Big question: What is a 'happiness curriculum', and should every school have one?

Getting started

Why do we ask questions? Questions play an essential role both in your education and personal life. Asking the right questions helps you to make sense of things and develop your understanding – and leads to new questions.

1. Work with a partner to think of as many reasons as you can why you ask questions in school. It might help you to think about the kinds of questions you ask:

   • yourself

   • your friends or other students

   • school teachers, tutors or other school staff

   • search engines, websites, textbooks, newspapers or library books.

Exploring

There are lots of reasons you ask questions. For example, you probably agreed with your partner that you ask teachers to explain things you do not understand.

So how do you construct these questions? What are the key words that help you get what you want? For example, if you wanted to know the time of a train, it would not help to ask: 'Who is the driver?' or 'Where is the right platform?'.

2 Look at these question words and phrases. In each case, what sort of thing does the questioner want to find out? Write an explanation for each question term. Here is one example:

What

Who

Why

Where

How many

When

How

> 'What' questions are aimed at finding out a particular piece of information.
> For example: *What is the most popular subject in our school?*

3 Now, note down some simple questions to check your explanations work. For example:

- Question: '*How* do we carry out experiments safely in science lessons?'

- Question: '*Where* is the…?"

These are not the only question words you might use. Here are some others:

a) '*Can* school uniform improve children's behaviour?'

b) '*Should* mobile phones be banned in schools?'

c) '*Does* a longer school day improve exam results?'

The above questions are all **closed questions**. They help you to develop your own **viewpoint**. Asking closed questions usually means you need to find **evidence**. This evidence might lead you to say, for example:

> 'No, school uniform *doesn't* improve children's behaviour because…'

> 'Yes, mobile phones *should* be banned in schools because…'

4 Briefly discuss questions a–c above with a partner. For each question:

- What is your viewpoint? Do you and your partner agree?

- What evidence have you got to support your view?

Developing

The various questions you can ask are especially useful when you are doing **research**.

- 'can', 'should', 'does', 'why' and 'how' are big question words that usually mean you need to look at things in depth as part of your research. No single piece of information will be the answer. These are great questions for making you curious and helping you think about your own opinion.

- 'who', 'what', 'when', 'how many' and 'where' questions generally help you answer the 'can/why' questions. They lead you to single facts or more specific information that could provide evidence, for example.

You could think of your big question as being at the top of a pyramid. Then your information questions come underneath, with the more important questions first.

Key terms

research: investigating an issue or topic to find out more about it

Vocabulary

curriculum: a teaching programme or set of plans

Key terms

source: a reference text or other form of information

Big question:
What is a 'happiness **curriculum**', and should every school have one?

'Why did India introduce a 'happiness curriculum'?

What is the 'happiness curriculum'?

When was it introduced and by whom?

Why was it introduced?   How will it affect schools?   Was it successful?

5   Look at this paragraph from an educational website. Which of the questions from the pyramid are answered in this **source**? Note down the answers.

www.edu…

In 2018, the Indian government introduced the Happiness Curriculum. The government said public schools should introduce meditation and mental exercises into the curriculum, in the form of a 45-minute daily 'happiness' session. This was to tackle the issue of students' well-being. Research showed that students were being put under huge pressure to achieve by parents, teachers and fellow learners.

School students in Maharashtra, India.

This leads to the most important question of all when creating your own research question: *What are you trying to find out?* If you are coming up with your own 'big' research question, then you need to be clear about:

- your topic or chosen issue
- your particular focus
- what you want to find out
- whether it is something you can find information on.

For example, a good question to ask if researching students' well-being might be: 'Should all schools introduce a happiness curriculum?'

- 'Should' indicates this is a closed question – you are looking for a definite answer (yes/no).
- 'Schools' is the focus of your research (not colleges or universities).
- 'Happiness curriculum' narrows the focus further – it is about the subjects taught, not the school buildings, for example.

Final task

6 You have been asked to research the issue of students' well-being in your school. You could think about the curriculum, the school environment, the school timetable and so on.

   a) Write down one 'big question' (a question that starts with 'Does/Should/Would').

   b) Write down three 'small', more analytical questions that might help you in your research.

? REFLECTION POINT

What questions could you ask to find out if a 'happiness curriculum' would work in your school? Write down at least one 'What' question and at least one 'Why' question.

Keep notes of your answers as part of building towards the final task in this chapter.

Identifying relevant sources and information

Skills focus
✓ Research
Learning focus
• Identify and begin to reference a range of sources.
• Locate information and answer research questions.

Big question: What would be a good design for a future school?

Getting started

How would you go about researching the big question above?
One way would be to think about what schools are like now.

1. Draw a map or diagram of your school in 10 minutes. Label as many parts of it as you can. Do not worry if you find drawing hard. This is just a quick task to get you thinking about schools and how they are designed.

Exploring

A student in the UK is using a **search engine** to answer the research question: 'What would be a good design for a school of the future?' These are the first three entries they find.

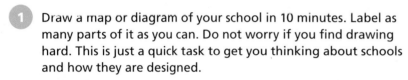

> What would be a good design for a school of the future?   × | ⚲
>
> www.schoolsforthefuture.co.uk
> ### Schools for the future
> **Schools** for the **Future** is an ambitious, long-term programme to raise education standards in Central Bedfordshire by ensuring the area has the right **schools**, in the right places, delivering the best education.
>
> www.typekids.com>blog>schools-of-the-future
> ### Schools for the future. – TypeKids
> Technology has never moved at such a fast pace. How can schools benefit from these developments? What should the **school** of the **future** look like?
>
> www.greenschool.org>insights>world economic forum
> ### World Economic Forum: Schools of the Future, 2020
> '**Schools of the Future**: Defining New Models of **Education** for the Fourth Industrial Revolution' outlines a new framework for defining quality education in the new economic and social context.

Based on Google search engine results.

2 Work in a group to match these notes made by the student to the search engine entries.

> **a)** Sounds complicated, but it does mention 'Green School'.
>
> **b)** Seems to be about exam results and *where* schools are built, not about design.
>
> **c)** Aimed at younger people and talks about 'technology'. Could be useful as technology is an important part of school design.

3 Working on your own, note down the source that you consider the most useful for researching ideas about designing 'schools of the future'. Give one reason.

When you decide whether a source is useful, you might consider:

- the vocabulary: are there words or phrases clearly linked to the topic you are researching?
- the information: are there facts, data or other details that could support a particular viewpoint?

Web searches like this produce lots of results. By reading the short description under the address and title – the 'snippet' – you can get an idea of what the content is. However, you do not really know until you open the link.

The student decides to look more closely at the third search result.

- They open the link.
- They **scroll down** and find information about the 'Green School'.
- Then, they **scan** the text to look for anything that mentions 'buildings', 'designs' or words related to these topics.

Here are some of the words and phrases the student picked out from the web article.

Indonesia Green School

Classrooms at Indonesia Green School in Bali.

The school's physical space supports critical thinking, creativity and **entrepreneurship**.

Learning takes place in a completely natural and **sustainable** environment that includes wall-less classrooms and a structure built entirely out of bamboo. The BioBus, a cooking-oil-fuelled vehicle designed by Green School students that saves over four tons of **carbon emissions** per year, transports students to and from school. The campus includes an **Innovation** Hub – a maker's space with woodworking equipment, 3D printers and laser engravers – and a Project Hub, where students **pitch** project ideas to be used in the classroom.

The school's location is integral for enabling students to connect directly with nature and consider ways to help the planet. In the early years, for example, children spend a significant portion of their time in the gardens and kitchen, developing **empathy** for nature and a general awareness about where their food is sourced. All students help maintain a sustainable environment in the school, and in the 2017–2018 school year produced over 150 kg of edible produce per month.

Source: Green School International © 2020.

4   List any other words or phrases in the web article about Green School that are related to the physical space (the design) of the school.

5   Write down at least three factual details provided (related to the design or environment).

6   Discuss in a small group:

   a) Is the source a relevant one?

   b) Does it provide any ideas you could use in designing your own school of the future?

Vocabulary

entrepreneurship: creative business ideas

sustainable: able to maintain natural resources at a certain level

carbon emissions: release of carbon dioxide due to human activity

innovation: new method or improvement

pitch: put forward for consideration

empathy: understanding

Developing

Web articles are only one type of source you might use in your research. Another student did an image search. They used the words 'future school design'. They were searching for photos of actual schools. Here is one they found of the Chaoyang Future School in Beijing, China.

Chaoyang Future School in Beijing.

7 Is this image a useful source to help you think about the design of future schools?

a) Does the image show the design of a school?

b) What do you think the people who designed the school were aiming to achieve?

c) Is the school 'futuristic' in any way? Or is it very similar to schools you already know?

Final task

8 Do your own online search using the term 'future school design' (or similar).

- Select three of the search returns and look at the 'snippets' (the short descriptions underneath).

- Choose the one that is most relevant and follow the link. Check out any text or images on the page.

- Write brief notes stating whether the source is useful and summarising any ideas for future school design it has given you. (Keep notes of your answers as part of building towards the final task in this chapter.)

? REFLECTION POINT

Conduct further research into Chaoyang Future School in Beijing, China. Would it be a school you would like to attend? Why?

Conducting research

Skills focus
✓ Research
Learning focus
• Select an appropriate research method.
• Conduct research to test predictions.

Big question: What are different people's views of what a school of the future should look like?

Getting started

1   Imagine there are plans to rebuild your school (even if it is new!). Spend 5 minutes listing all the different groups of people you could **interview** to get their opinion on what the new, rebuilt school should look like.

Exploring

Interviewing is just one research method. Here are some others.

Experiments (**in the field** or laboratory)	Observation (for example, of people)
Questionnaires and **surveys**	Internet search
Checking reports, graphs and data	Library research

These types of research are usually divided into two categories: **primary** and **secondary** research.

2   Which of these research methods have you used before?

    a) What was the situation? Was it part of a school subject, for example?

    b) What were you trying to find out?

    c) Was your research primary or secondary?

It is important to think about how each research method will be useful. For example, using a web search to find out what other students feel about something today is unlikely to help you. You might need primary research – asking students yourself.

🔑 Key terms

interview: a conversation in which one person asks another person questions

in the field: a particular location where research is carried out

questionnaire: a written set of questions requiring a response

survey: to ask a series of questions to find out information about a particular subject

primary research: research you do yourself, for example interviewing people

secondary research: research done using other people's research findings

You also need to make other decisions when conducting research.

- For example, in a questionnaire you could choose to use closed questions, **open questions** or **multiple-choice** questions.

- When you conduct research, it is often to test a **prediction**.

Three students made predictions about what features their parents would want a new school to include.

Hanni:	Well, I think the majority of parents will say sports facilities must be included.
Xin:	Hmm. Maybe. I think most parents will expect the school to be built of sustainable materials.
Kendra:	I think no one will want open-plan classrooms. Parents expect traditional, individual classrooms with rows of desks.

The students' class gave out a questionnaire to parents. One of the questions asked them to choose the three most important features for a new school. Here are the responses of 100 parents.

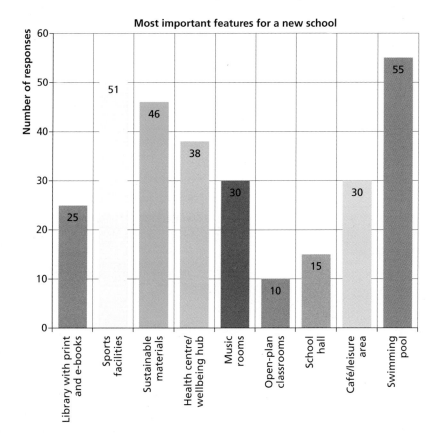

Most important features for a new school

3 a) Whose predictions were correct?

b) Whose predictions were incorrect?

c) Which feature for the new school was most popular?

d) Which feature was least popular?

Developing

Research methods can also be divided in two other ways:

- **Quantitative**: the answers can be measured. For example, like the graph in the previous lessson, you can find out a specific number of parents who voted for music rooms as an important feature (in this case, 30 parents).

- **Qualitative**: the answers tell you how people or groups feel, or what their opinions are. A question such as 'How would you feel if your child's school did not have a traditional library?' could help you understand why people made a particular choice or why some features were seen as important (or not).

The three students showed parents the photo of the Green School from Unit 2.2 and asked them: 'What are your thoughts about a school made of sustainable materials and with a focus on the environment?' Here are some of their responses:

Parent A:	I'm more interested in what my child will be taught than what the school is built from!
Parent B:	It's not practical. Our winters are far too cold. My child will freeze if the school is made of bamboo and straw.
Parent C:	It's a great idea. It sends the message that you must care for the environment.
Parent D:	I'm in favour of it in principle, but won't it be too expensive?

As you can see, the parents give four very different perspectives – each with a reason.

4   The responses above can lead to both qualitative *and* quantitative responses. For example, note down answers to these questions:

a) Of the four parents, how many are definitely in favour?

b) What are the different concerns expressed by some parents?

c) Which of questions a and b would get a qualitative response?

Final task

Key terms

stakeholder: someone with a specific interest or involvement in something

5 Work in a group of 4 or 5 students to conduct further research about the school of the future and its design. You want to find out more about what key **stakeholders** think about:

- materials (what the building should be made of)
- location (where it would ideally be built, for example in the middle of a city)
- structure and organisation (levels, floors, shapes)
- the 'feel' or mood of the building (for example, calm, business-like, collaborative)
- classrooms (for example, traditional, digital).

a) Each person in the group chooses one of these categories. Write down a prediction for how you think 10 teachers you ask might respond in this area. For example: 'I believe most teachers will prefer a regular, rectangular-based classroom design or structure.'

b) Then, decide how you will test your prediction. Write down the method you would use (for example, questionnaire) and whether it is quantitative or qualitative. Use this basic grid.

My category	My prediction	My chosen method?	Quantitative or qualitative?

c) Finally, set up your research method and carry out your research.

❓ REFLECTION POINT

How are your own ideas of a 'future school' taking shape? How has the research you have done so far changed or confirmed any ideas you have had?

Using the five elements above (materials, location, structure, mood, classrooms) note down your own personal ideas, giving a reason for each choice.

Evaluating sources

Skills focus
✓ Evaluation
Learning focus
- Understand an author's purpose in a source.
- Make a judgement about whether a source is biased.

Big question: Should schools get rid of traditional subjects (such as mathematics, science and history)?

Getting started

1   Talk with a partner about your school subjects. List at least one 'real world' application for each of them. For example, for mathematics, this could be working out how much paint you might use to paint a room in your house.

Exploring

Once you have identified a potentially useful source, you need to **evaluate** it. As part of this process, you need to recognise when someone makes an **assertion** or uses **bias**. Consider this example:

> Rostin Academy is the worst school in the area.
>
> Goldstar College is a high-achieving school, unlike Rostin Academy. It has a 65% pass rate for English and Maths.

— This is an assertion.

— This is an opinion, containing bias. No evidence is presented about Rostin Academy's results, which might be higher.

Even if a source contains bias, this does not mean it is not useful. However, you need to recognise that there might be other views and evidence that has been ignored.

2   Read the following article from a local paper. Identify:

a) at least one assertion (a statement made without evidence)

b) an example of bias (a statement that ignores any contrasting evidence).

Rostin Academy's popularity drops

In the past year, Rostin Academy's popularity has dropped among parents. What is more, students' behaviour has deteriorated compared with other local schools. Five per cent of all students at Rostin Academy were excluded for at least one day over the course of the school year. Clearly, discipline is not what it should be.

🔑 Key terms

evaluate: make a judgement about something's worth or effectiveness

bias: favouring one person or point of view over another in a way considered to be unfair

assertion: a claim made without supporting evidence

Developing

Your group has been trying to answer the big question at the start of this unit: 'Should schools get rid of traditional subjects (such as mathematics, science and history)?'

One of your group has found this source. Read it carefully.

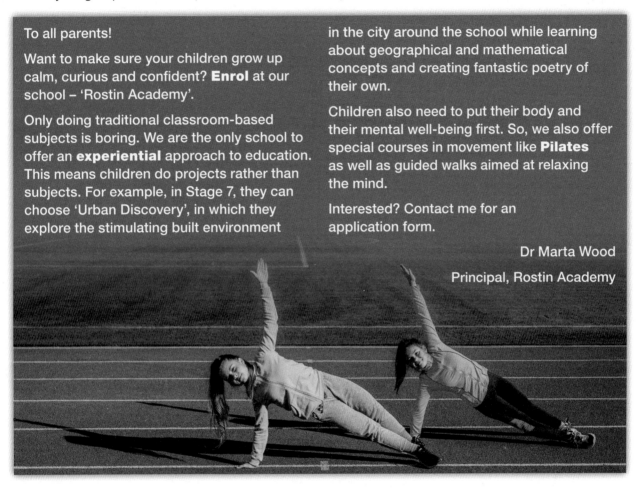

To all parents!

Want to make sure your children grow up calm, curious and confident? **Enrol** at our school – 'Rostin Academy'.

Only doing traditional classroom-based subjects is boring. We are the only school to offer an **experiential** approach to education. This means children do projects rather than subjects. For example, in Stage 7, they can choose 'Urban Discovery', in which they explore the stimulating built environment in the city around the school while learning about geographical and mathematical concepts and creating fantastic poetry of their own.

Children also need to put their body and their mental well-being first. So, we also offer special courses in movement like **Pilates** as well as guided walks aimed at relaxing the mind.

Interested? Contact me for an application form.

Dr Marta Wood

Principal, Rostin Academy

To judge whether a source is biased, you need to understand:

- the author of the source
- the audience for the source
- the purpose of the source
- what the source is about.

3   Work as a group to discuss answers to these questions about the author, audience and purpose of the source above. Note down your answers.

   a) Who has written it?

   b) Who is it aimed at? (Who is meant to read it?)

   c) Why did the author write this source? Did they have a **vested interest**? If so, what?

Vocabulary

enrol: sign up for

experiential: based on experiencing something yourself

Pilates: a movement programme designed to improve strength, posture and mental awareness

vested interest: a personal reason for involvement in or support of something

4 Next, make notes about the source itself:

    a) What does the author have to say about 'traditional' subjects?

    b) What factual information does the author give about Stage 7 and the 'special courses' on offer?

    c) What opinion does the author give about children's bodies and 'mental well-being'?

5 Now, evaluate the source:

    a) What are the strengths and weaknesses of the source? Does it help you answer the question about traditional subjects?

    b) What else might you need to research to evaluate the school's approach more fully? (For example, could you compare examination results with other schools?)

Final task

It is important to find other sources with different perspectives.

Read the extract from a newspaper article below.

> ## Vocabulary
>
> **discredited**: something that people no longer respect or that is considered less acceptable
>
> **anecdotal**: based on brief, personal accounts rather than facts or evidence

Education study finds in favour of traditional teaching styles

by Richard Adams

Schools need to put more effort into evaluating what makes effective teaching, and ensure that **discredited** practices are rooted out from classrooms, according to a new study published by the Sutton Trust and Durham University.

The study suggests that some schools and teachers continue using methods that cause little or no improvement in student progress, and instead rely on **anecdotal** evidence to back fashionable techniques such as 'discovery learning,' where pupils are meant to uncover key ideas for themselves, or 'learning styles,' which claims children can be divided into those who learn best through sight, sound or movement.

Instead, more traditional styles that reward effort, use class time efficiently and insist on clear rules to manage pupil behaviour, are more likely to succeed, according to the report.

Source: *The Guardian*, 31 October 2014.

6 Evaluate the source by writing answers to these questions.

a) Who is the author of this source? What job or role do they have?

b) What sort of text is it? What is its purpose?

c) When was it written? (How might this affect the source's validity?)

d) What facts – if any – does the source contain?

e) What viewpoint or perspective is expressed? Is this the author's viewpoint – or someone else's?

f) Does the author of the article have a vested interest in 'traditional' or 'non-traditional' approaches?

g) Is there anything in the article that could help you decide whether one of these approaches is better than the other?

h) What further research might you have to do?

❓ REFLECTION POINT

It is useful to keep track of what you learn about your own skills or ideas by keeping a log. For example, add notes on your ideas about how schools of the future should look.

• How have any of the new sources you have looked at here affected your views (if at all)?

• How might teaching styles and approaches (for example, discovery learning) affect how a school building might be designed?

Recording your findings

Skills focus
✓ Research
Learning focus
• Select relevant information from sources.
• Organise and record the information.

Big question: Should students themselves be the ones who decide what they learn?

Getting started

When you are looking to solve a problem, it helps to be able to refer to clear, informative notes.

1. Discuss with a partner the ways you make notes in school.

   How and when do you make notes? Think of three different subject areas, and how you record ideas or work out solutions.

Exploring

It is likely that whatever note-making format you use, most of it will be written down. It can be useful to record your thoughts in other ways (such as voice memos on a phone), but at some point you may need to check back. Checking can be easier when your notes are written down.

When you first work with a source, your notes can be quite 'free'. You can make use of highlighting, labelling or **annotating**. For example, look again at part of the source from Unit 2.4.

> 🔑 **Key terms**
>
> **annotating**: adding notes to text or a diagram to explain or comment on its features

Only doing traditional classroom-based subjects is boring. — Only an assertion – many people like doing traditional subjects.

We are the only school to offer an experiential approach — What does this term mean, exactly?
to education. This means children do projects rather than subjects. For example, in Stage 7, they can choose
'Urban Discovery', in which they explore the stimulating
built environments around the school while learning about — OK, so this is what a 'project' is.
geographical and mathematical concepts. and creating
fantastic poetry of their own. — Persuasive language about the work they do.

2 Read the school timetable below, from the Rostin Academy website, and make your own notes about it. You could:

- highlight anything you do not understand or want to know more about

- add comments – like the annotations on the source above.

- note down whether you think the source is useful or relevant in answering the big question – is this the type of school where students decide what they learn?

Monday Timetable, Rostin Academy	
7:00–8:00 a.m.	Breakfast in the Urban Lookout Tower
8:00–8:15 a.m.	Registration in class
8:15–11:00 a.m.	Urban Discovery Project: Maths and Geography challenges
11:00–11:30 a.m.	Break
11:30–1:00 p.m.	Well-being choice: Pilates or tree-top ropeway walk
1:00–2:00 p.m.	Lunch
2:00–3:30 p.m.	Free choice: creative writing, games, sport, art
3:30 p.m.	End of school
3:30–4:30 p.m.	Homework Hub

Developing

After you have made your initial annotations, it can be helpful to record them in a more systematic way. For example, you could record:

- the date you made the notes or the date of the source

- the source details: who wrote it, the format (for example, a report), audience and purpose (if relevant)

- any key details or facts from it

- whether it is biased in any way

- questions or further actions you need to take.

Here is one way a student has recorded their thoughts on the leaflet about Rostin Academy in Unit 2.4.

Date found	20 October
Source	Leaflet for Rostin Academy
Author	Principal, Dr Marta Wood
Audience	Parents
Purpose	To persuade parents to send children to the school
Features/details	Discovery projects, not single subjects; well-being choice
Perspective	Possible bias and/or vested interest, as she is Principal
My notes	How can I check out what others think about the school?

3 Look at the table below. Complete as many parts of it as you can based on the Rostin Academy timetable. The table has been started for you. You may find some parts cannot be completed due to lack of information.

Date found	20 October
Source	
Author	Rostin Academy
Audience	
Purpose	
Features/details	Breakfast in Urban Lookout Tower
Perspective	n/a
My notes	Is enough time devoted to 'traditional' learning?

When making notes, it can be helpful to use common **abbreviations** (for example, 'intro' for 'introduction', 'v' for 'very', 'n/a' for 'not applicable', and so on) and leave out articles or other non-essential words. For example: *Is (there) enough time devoted to trad(itional) learning?*

Final task

4 Read the extract from a newspaper article on the opposite page.

   a) Make initial notes on a copy of the article. You could:

   • highlight or underline anything you do not understand or want to know more about

   • add comments giving your own thoughts and evaluating the source (as in Unit 2.4).

   b) Complete a log entry recording the main details about this source, using a table like the one above.

   c) In the 'My Notes' section, add a comment about how primary research could help you find out more about the issues raised.

Ocean Island Times
by Maisie Roper,
21 May 2023

Is that a student or a teacher?

Student teaching other students maths.

At our local high school, a revolution in learning is taking place. Standing at the front of the class of 13–14-year-olds is another student. She is teaching the rest of the class how to factorise a quadratic equation – and she is doing it brilliantly. The class have their heads down and are making notes. At the end, she tests them and checks their understanding. This is just one of the ways the school is looking to turn around its performance, after regularly underperforming in the local area test results.

'We realised the students needed to own their own learning,' the Principal explains. 'So, we asked them what they wanted more and less of. Then, we built a curriculum that was flexible so some students could choose to do more mathematics if they wanted to. We have also stopped punishing students for non-attendance. Instead, we seek to find out why and give them opportunities to do the things they want to. Children miss school when they do not like what they are learning. Give them what they want, and there is no reason to stay away,' she says. It all sounds very impressive.

❓ REFLECTION POINT

You have used a log to record your comments on sources. Now try using a simple table to begin to focus your ideas about a 'future school'. For example:

Overall style or teaching approach	Traditional, disciplined, academic subjects because…
Curriculum/timetable	Hour-long lessons because…
School design/layout	Cubed rooms, long corridors because…

Applying what you have learned

Skills focus
✓ Evaluation
✓ Communication
Learning focus
• Evaluate a range of sources.
• Communicate effectively.

Your task

Your group will create a short presentation called 'Our School of the Future'. It should include a plan of the school and slides explaining your ideas.

Approaching the task

Look over the notes you have made so far, including the table you completed at the end of Unit 2.5. You will need to comment on three aspects in your presentation:

• Your future school's overall shape, materials and design: how do these fit with the school's aims (for example, to promote academic excellence and discipline)?

• The school's surroundings/outside areas: what will they look like? How will they support the school's aims?

• The curriculum/timetable: what will be taught? What will a typical school day look like? How does the building design support this?

Here is a plan for the Chaoyang Future School. Your plan does not have to be so detailed, but this will give you an idea of the sort of thing you could produce, and what you could say. For example, how does the plan below encourage collaborative working?

(1) **Open Learning Zone** 开放教学区
(2) **Leisure & Discussion Zone** 休闲讨论区
(3) **Classrooms** 教室
(4) **Reading Room** 阅览室
(5) **Activity Room** 综合活动室
(6) **Bathroom** 卫生间

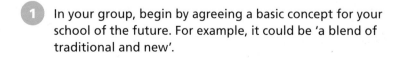

LEARNING CENTER F5
学习中心 五层

0 2 6 14m

Figure 2.6.1: Plan of the Learning Center at Chaoyang Future School.

(1) In your group, begin by agreeing a basic concept for your school of the future. For example, it could be 'a blend of traditional and new'.

2 Next, allocate different roles to each member of your group. For example:

- planner/designer (responsible for creating the plan)
- curriculum expert (responsible for what is taught and how)
- builder/architect (responsible for the buildings)
- landscape designer (responsible for the outdoor environments).

3 Each team member now works on their own aspect (the drawing may need to be done in stages as each other aspect is completed).

4 As you work on your chosen area, create a draft slide that sums up your suggestions. Where appropriate, refer to any sources from this chapter that affected your thinking.

5 You may want to add illustrations or images. If you need to, create a second slide for these.

6 Then, share your draft slides with your group. Listen to any suggestions they have and, if needed, make changes. Then redraft and finish your slides.

7 Come back together as a group. Decide the order for the presentation, and whether you need an introduction and conclusion. You will also need to agree a name for your school that reflects its **ethos**.

8 Finally, your group presents its ideas to another group or the rest of the class.

Key terms

ethos: aims and values

Checklist for success

- ✔ Introduce your overall idea clearly and simply.
- ✔ Speak clearly when it is your turn.
- ✔ Give reasons for your suggestions.
- ✔ Avoid reading word for word from your notes. Instead, use speaking prompts.
- ✔ End by asking the class if they have any questions.

Reflecting on your progress

What have you learned about researching and evaluating sources? Look at the checklist on the next page and independently select the skills you think you have mastered. Then, with a partner, discuss:

- any new skills you have learned
- what you need to improve
- how the process has helped you to develop your thinking about an issue.

Check your progress

Beginning	Developing	Going beyond
• I can break down a research question to prepare for answering it.	• I can use a range of question types for different purposes.	• I can use wider, issue-based questions and more analytical ones.
• I can carry out a web search using a key term and make a basic judgement of the responses.	• I can select the most relevant result to follow up from a web search.	• I can scan the most relevant results from a web search for further information.
• I can use at least one research method to find out information.	• I can select information from qualitative and quantitative research methods.	• I select information from primary and secondary research methods and qualitative and quantitative results.
• I recognise opinion and bias in a source.	• I evaluate sources according to a range of criteria, including assertion and bias.	• I draw on a wide range of criteria to evaluate sources.
• I record my thoughts and ideas by making basic notes.	• I make notes and transfer relevant ones to a useful log.	• I keep detailed, useful notes and logs to guide my research.

Next steps

- Think about developing a standard template of your own for recording sources for research work you do.

- Conduct your own research into how schools have changed over the last century or so. You could create a basic timeline and for every 20 years, paste an image of a school (perhaps your own, if it is an old one) and show how it has changed. Or you could explore school designs in another country.

Identifying ideas and evidence

A billion heartbeats in a lifetime?

3

Many animals have a life expectancy of a billion heartbeats, but humans are an exception, reaching well over double that. How have we managed this, and will we continue to live longer and longer?

In this chapter, you will be exploring the topic 'Health and wellbeing', thinking about the following issues:

- **Will a slower heart rate mean a longer life?**

- **Why has human life expectancy increased?**

- **Do people in wealthier countries live longer?**

- **If you were running a country, how could you increase people's life expectancy?**

- **Will yours be the first generation to live to be 100?**

You will be developing a range of research and evaluation skills:

3.1 Analysing data to identify patterns and trends

3.2 Explaining trends in data

3.3 Seeing if the evidence supports an argument

3.4 Selecting actions to address an issue

3.5 Exploring predictions about the future

3.6 Applying what you have learned.

When you study the evidence in this chapter, you will see that human life expectancy has changed over time at different rates in different places. The reasons for this are varied; the focus in this chapter is on how governments can improve life expectancy rather on than exploring why there are historical differences. Your final task will be to use ideas you have developed over the chapter to suggest the most effective way a country could increase the life expectancy of its citizens.

Analysing data to identify patterns and trends

Skills focus
✓ Analysis

Learning focus
- Analyse data to identify patterns and trends.
- Suggest correlations between sets of data.
- Use evidence to support conclusions.

Big question: Will a slower heart rate mean a longer life?

Getting started

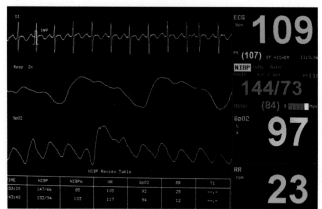

1 Imagine someone has been rushed into **intensive care** in a hospital. They are connected to a **monitor** and the screen looks like this image.

a) Why do you think the person has been connected to a monitor?

b) One of the lines on the screen shows **heart rate**. Which colour line do you think it is?

c) Why is it considered essential to monitor heart rate?

d) How useful is this information to understand the condition of the patient?

Exploring

The information shown on the hospital monitor is displayed in both **numerical** and **graphical** form. The numerical form gives an accurate reading at that point in time, and the graphical form shows the pattern over time.

Heart rate is of interest to more than just medical experts – it's one of the factors that indicates wellbeing. People can use heart rate to investigate stress and fitness.

2 Find your own **pulse** – with a bit of practice, you can do this at the wrist and the neck. Make sure you use your fingers rather than thumb (as the thumb has its own pulse). Use a watch or timer and count the number of beats in 15 seconds.

a) How many heartbeats did you count in 15 seconds?

b) Calculate from this what your heart rate is in beats per minute and record this.

c) What might cause your heart rate to vary?

Vocabulary

intensive care: part of a hospital in which people who are very ill receive special treatment

monitor: screen that displays information, for example from a computer

heart rate: the number of times a person's heart beats in one minute

pulse: the rhythmic beat of the heart felt in the blood vessels of the wrist and neck

🔑 Key terms

numerical: information given in the form of numbers

graphical: information given in the form of a graph

3 The heart rate for a typical 9–12-year-old at rest (that is, when not being physically active) is 84 beats per minute (bpm). However, resting heart rate for 9–12-year-olds can vary from 52 to 115 beats per minute.

a) Compare your results for resting heart rate within the class. Did anyone in the group get 84 beats per minute?

b) What is the average resting heart rate for the class?

c) What conclusion can you draw from measuring data in this way?

d) Why is there such a wide range in heart rates? Is this useful information?

e) How accurate is your data on heart rate as a class? For example, did everyone take the readings in the same way?

It is possible to measure the heart rates of many different animals. The table shows how some of them compare.

4 Work with a partner to answer these questions.

a) How do these heart rates compare with yours?

b) Draw a bar chart to show how the heart rates of the animals in the table compare. Include yourself on the chart as well.

c) Looking at your chart, which type of animal seems to have a higher heart rate and which a lower heart rate?

d) Use the chart to predict the heart rates of:

- a horse

- a sheep

- a mouse.

e) Suggest why a bar chart is a good way of displaying and analysing this type of information.

f) Why might the data for some animals be more accurate than for others?

g) Based on the data in your chart, what do you think the relationship is between animals and life expectancy?

Animal	Heart rate
Blue whale	8–10 bpm
African elephant	25–35 bpm
Dolphin	35–45 bpm
Condor	65 bpm

Table 3.1.1: Heart rates of different animals.

Developing

Does a lower heart rate (fewer heartbeats per minute) mean a longer life? In other words, is there a **correlation** between heart rate and **longevity**?

To answer this question, you will need to analyse more data to see if there is a pattern. If different sources present similar information, this will give you the **evidence** you need to reach a conclusion.

Let's start by looking at the data in the table.

Animal	Mass (kg)	Heart rate (bpm)	Life expectancy (years)	Lifetime heartbeats (billions)
Horse	1200	44	40	0.93
Cow	800	65	22	0.75
Human	90	60	70	2.21
Monkey	5	190	15	1.50
Cat	2	150	15	1.18
Chicken	1.5	275	15	2.17
Rabbit	1	205	9	0.97

Table 3.1.2: Data about different animals.

 5 Which of these statements are supported by the data in the table?

a) The animals further up the table are bigger than the animals lower down.

b) Smaller animals have a shorter life expectancy.

c) The lower the heart rate, the longer the life expectancy.

d) All the animals shown have hearts that beat about the same number of times over their lifespan.

Let's now explore the idea that all animals have a similar number of heartbeats in their lifetimes. This would mean that the slower the heart rate, the longer the life. Examining the data for individual animals should tell you if this is true.

The graph on the next page is plotted for life expectancy (in years) against heart rate (in beats per minute).

On the graph, the curved line shows where an animal would appear if its lifespan consisted of a billion heartbeats. Any animal that plots above the line will have more than a billion heartbeats in its life, and any animal that plots below the line will have fewer than a billion heartbeats.

🔑 Key terms

correlation: relationship or connection between two or more factors, for example heart rate and life expectancy

evidence: facts and information that can be used to prove whether something is true

Vocabulary

longevity: length of life

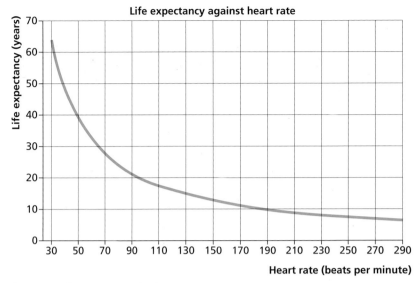

Figure 3.1.3: Life expectancy against heart rate.

Final task

It is important when you are offering an idea that you can demonstrate that it is supported by evidence. It is the evidence that will either show the idea to be **valid** or undermine it.

6　**a)** Use the data in Table 3.1.2 to plot points on the life expectancy against heart rate graph for all the animals.

　　b) How close are the animals to the line? Comment on each animal.

　　c) Is it true to say that most animals are on the line or close to it?

　　d) Do humans fit this **trend**?

　　e) The average human heart rate is 60 beats per minute. Use the graph to find out what the life expectancy of a human would be if their heart lasted for a billion heartbeats.

7　Let's think about the role of data.

　　a) To what extent does the data support the idea that all animals get a billion heartbeats in their lives?

　　b) If none of the animals plotted on the graph is exactly on the line, does this mean that the idea is false? Why?

　　c) Humans are some way off the line and are getting over 2 billion heartbeats per lifetime. What might explain this?

❓ REFLECTION POINT

Consider how you explored the ideas in this unit.

* Why was it essential to have data?

* How well did the evidence support the ideas?

Explaining trends in data

Skills focus
✓ Evaluation
Learning focus
- Suggest patterns and trends in data.
- Identify limitations with the quality of data.
- Use evidence to suggest where various claims may or may not be supported.

Big question: Why has human life expectancy increased?

Getting started

Humans haven't always had two billion heartbeats in their lifetime. In the past, human life expectancy was much less than it is now, and humans were living lives that lasted for around a billion heartbeats.

1 **a)** Why do you think that human life expectancy used to be shorter than it is now?

b) Why do you think people today live for longer?

Exploring

This unit will put forward **arguments** about life expectancy and how it has changed. Evidence will be used to support those arguments.

Look at this map of the world, which shows the average life expectancy in each continent in the year 1800.

> **🔑 Key terms**
>
> **argument:** a series of statements containing reasons and evidence which support a claim about a global issue

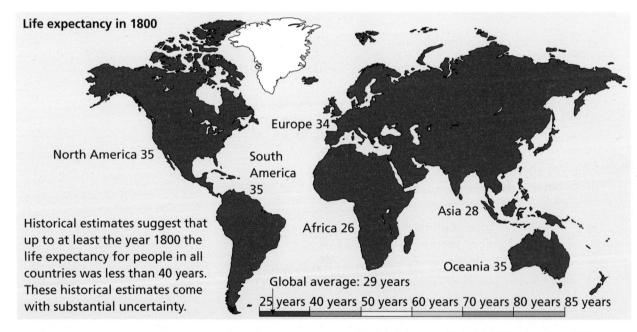

Life expectancy in 1800

North America 35
Europe 34
South America 35
Africa 26
Asia 28
Oceania 35

Historical estimates suggest that up to at least the year 1800 the life expectancy for people in all countries was less than 40 years. These historical estimates come with substantial uncertainty.

Global average: 29 years

25 years 40 years 50 years 60 years 70 years 80 years 85 years

Figure 3.2.1: Life expectancy in 1800.
Source: Based on data from Our World in Data. Map redrawn by Collins Bartholomew.

Whenever you look at information like this, you need to think about where the data came from and how accurate it is. In some countries, records are kept of the dates of births and deaths of individual people. Some countries have graveyards where some people are buried, and their age is shown on headstones.

2 **a)** Why might gathering data from gravestones not necessarily give an accurate representation of life expectancy overall in that part of the world?

b) Why might written records in some countries not be complete?

c) Why might wealthier people be more strongly represented in the data than poorer people?

d) Why might some people have tried to avoid attempts by their governments to gather data about births and deaths?

3 The world map does give some indication of life expectancy.

a) Suggest an overall conclusion from the map.

b) Look at the detail on the key. What was the global average life span?

c) Does the map suggest that nobody lived over the age of 40? Why?

We could make the argument that, in 1800, all continents had an average life expectancy of less than 40 years. While the evidence in the map seems to support this argument, as you have seen, there are limitations with the quality of the data. However, the evidence can be interpreted in more than one way.

4 Consider these two **interpretations** of why life expectancy in Asia in 1800 was 28 years.

> The map shows that life expectancy in Asia in 1800 was 28 years. This was because people lived until their late 20s and then died. So, their life expectancy was limited by the work they did or the conditions under which women gave birth.

> It could be that many people in Asia lived longer than 28 years, but the average could be low because of poor **infant mortality rates**. In other words, the problem wasn't lots of people dying in their 20s and 30s. Instead, it was lots of people dying as children.

a) Which interpretation do you think is more likely, and why?

b) What type of evidence could help you decide?

> **Key terms**
>
> **interpretation**: an explanation or opinion as to why something is a certain way

> **Vocabulary**
>
> **infant mortality rate**: the number of children who die under the age of 1 out of 1000 live births

Developing

The map shows data about global life expectancy in 1950.

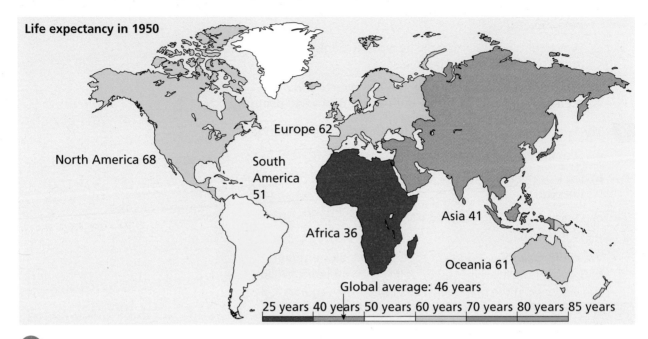

Life expectancy in 1950

Europe 62

North America 68

South America 51

Africa 36

Asia 41

Oceania 61

Global average: 46 years

25 years 40 years 50 years 60 years 70 years 80 years 85 years

Figure 3.2.2: Life expectancy in 1950.
Source: Based on Our World in Data data taken from the United Nations Population Division country estimates in 1950. Map redrawn by Collins Bartholomew.

5 Compare the map showing life expectancy in 1950 with the one for 1800.

   a) Which continents show a considerable increase in life expectancy?

   b) Which continents show a small increase in life expectancy?

   c) Do you think the quality of data will have changed? Why/why not?

6 Read this interpretation on the right, based on the map showing life expectancy in 1950:

Does the evidence from the map support this interpretation? Remember to:

   • identify any patterns and trends in the data (how it has changed over time)

   • consider any limitations with the quality of data (how reliable is it?)

   • use evidence to suggest where the interpretation may or may not be supported.

> By 1950, the world had become a less equal place in terms of life expectancy.

7 Now look at the map on the next page showing life expectancy in 2015. Compare it with the map for 1950.

   a) What are the main changes between 1950 and 2015?

   b) Does the evidence shown in the maps support the statement on the right? You will need to:

   • Summarise the key points

   • Support your answer with reference to the evidence shown in the maps.

> In 1950, someone living in North America or Western Europe could expect to live until their mid-60s. The rest of the world enjoyed this level of life expectancy by 2015.

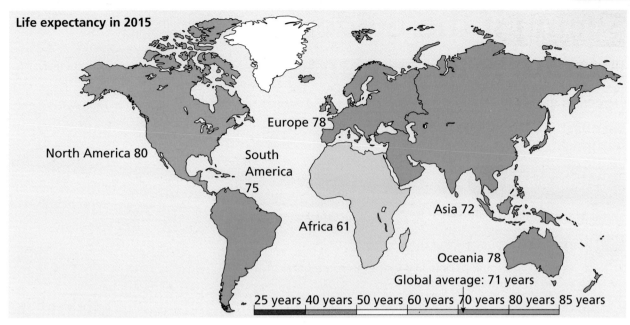

Figure 3.2.3: Life expectancy in 2015.
Source: Based on Our World in Data data taken from the United Nations Population Division country estimates in 2015. Map redrawn by Collins Bartholomew.

Final task

Throughout this unit, you have been looking at how evidence can support arguments. For an interpretation to be valid, it needs to be supported with evidence.

8 Using all the information in this unit, decide whether each of these statements is valid. Working with a partner, refer to the evidence from the maps and to the limitations of the data to support your answer in each case.

a) People in every continent had a higher life expectancy in 2015 than they did in 1950.

b) The quality of the data has improved from 1800 to 2015.

c) The gap in life expectancy between different parts of the world widened from 1800 to 1950 but then narrowed between 1950 and 2015.

d) There is less of a gap in life expectancy between different parts of the world in 2015 than there was in 1950.

e) By 2015, continents in the northern **hemisphere** had a higher life expectancy than those in the southern hemisphere.

> **Vocabulary**
>
> **hemisphere**: half of a sphere; refers to half of the Earth, which can be divided into northern and southern halves by the equator

❓ REFLECTION POINT

- Suggest why having data such as these world charts is essential to identify trends and evaluate interpretations.

- Why is it important to think about the quality of the data that you are working with?

Seeing if the evidence supports an argument

Skills focus
✓ Evaluation
Learning focus
- Discuss how good an argument is that has been presented.
- Explore the structure of an argument and how well evidence supports it.

Big question: Do people in wealthier countries live longer?

Getting started

In the previous unit, you looked at how life expectancy varies.

1 Working in a group, answer these questions.

a) Why do you think people live longer in some parts of the world than others?

List as many reasons as you can.

b) Suggest why the wealth of a country might enable its citizens to live longer. Make a list of possible reasons.

Exploring

The argument that you are going to explore in this unit is 'People who live in wealthier countries have longer and better lives'. Let's see what the evidence says.

A useful way to work out the wealth of a country is to use a measure called Gross Domestic Product (GDP). Put simply, this is the amount of money a country earns from things it makes and services it provides, divided by its population. GDP is the wealth generated per citizen.

In the graph below, life expectancy has been plotted against GDP **per capita**.

- Every country is shown as a dot. The size of each dot indicates the size of the population of that country, so, the larger the dot, the larger the population.

- The graph's vertical **axis** shows life expectancy, so the higher up the vertical scale the dot is, the greater the life expectancy for that country.

- The graph's horizontal axis shows GDP, so the wealthier a country is, the further the dot moves to the right.

🔑 Key terms

per capita: the total amount of something in a country divided by the number of people in the country

axis: a line on a graph showing a scale of measurement

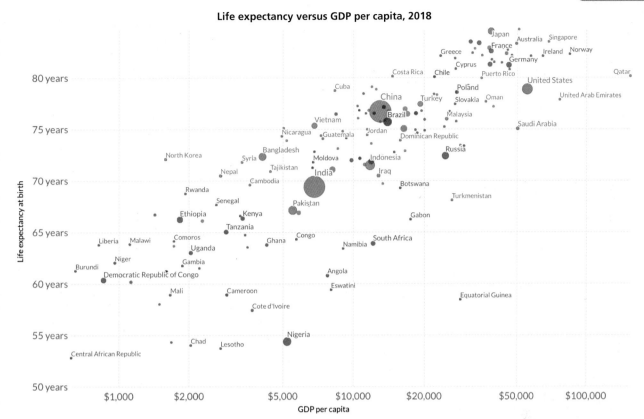

Figure 3.3.1: Life expectancy versus GDP per capita, 2018.
Source: Our World in Data.

Africa
Asia
Europe
North America
Oceania
South America

1:4B
600M

Dots sized by
Population

2 Where on the graph would a country appear if:

a) it was wealthy and its citizens had high life expectancy?

b) it was poor and its citizens had low life expectancy?

3 What would it tell you if:

a) a country's dot appeared in the upper left area of the graph?

b) a country's dot appeared in the lower right area of the graph?

4 Use the graph to name:

a) three countries with a high GDP whose citizens have a long life expectancy

b) three countries with a low GDP whose citizens have a shorter life expectancy.

5 The argument you are exploring in this unit is: greater wealth supports longer life expectancy. Think about your analysis of the evidence shown by the graph.

a) Does the graph show that this argument is always valid?

b) Does the argument have some truth but there are exceptions?

c) Could it be argued that the wealth of a country does not tell us anything about the life expectancy of its people?

Use evidence from the graph to support your answer in each case.

Developing

Let's now consider how life expectancy can be addressed.

6 Read the views expressed in these articles, and the information given. Then answer the questions that follow.

Life expectancy in low-income countries on the rise

by Kailey Dubinsky

Health aid has a high impact in low-income regions because many of the leading causes of death are easily preventable or treatable. Vaccines have all but wiped out the most deadly diseases in children including tetanus, polio and measles. For every billion dollars spent on health aid, around 364,800 deaths of children under five are prevented.

Source: The Borgen Project, 11 July 2017.

More education is what makes people live longer, not more money

by Debora Mackenzie

Wolfgang Lutz of the International Institute for Applied Systems Analysis in Vienna and colleagues have compiled average data on GDP per person, lifespans, and years of education from 174 countries, dating from 1970 to 2010.

Lutz argues that because schooling happens many years before a person has attained their life expectancy, this correlation reflects cause: better education drives longer life. It also tends to lead to more wealth, which is why wealth and longevity are also correlated. But what is important, says Lutz, is that wealth does not seem to be driving longevity, as experts thought – in fact, education is driving both of them.

Source: *New Scientist*, 18 April 2018.

a) What does each article identify as a key factor in life expectancy and why?

b) Why might we regard these sources as trustworthy? Read the following information.

- The Borgen Project is a non-government independent research organisation in the USA.

- *New Scientist* is a widely published and read scientific **journal**.

- The International Institute for Applied Systems Analysis in Vienna is a respected scientific organisation.

> **Vocabulary**
>
> **journal**: a publication or website that focuses on a particular area of speciality – here, science. In some journals, articles are peer reviewed, which means they have been checked by experts.

Final task

The **issue** of life expectancy is one that is important to people – they want to live long and healthy lives. It is also important as a global issue.

7 Work in a group of 4–6, and form two teams.

- Team A's job is to find evidence to support statements a–e below.

- Team B's job is to find evidence against each of the statements.

Both teams will need to look back at all the evidence in this chapter so far.

STATEMENTS

a) Every country in the world has seen an increase in life expectancy over the last 200 years.

b) The rank order of continents according to life expectancy hasn't altered over the last 200 years.

c) Life expectancy is related to wealth: the richer the country, the longer the people in it live.

d) The international variation in life expectancy has increased in the last 200 years.

e) Wealth is not a guarantee of living longer – some wealthy countries have a lower life expectancy.

❓ REFLECTION POINT

If countries are going to invest in ways of improving their life expectancy, they need to be basing this on evidence. This isn't always easy.

- How easy did you find it to analyse the evidence given in this unit and decide whether it supported the argument that wealthier countries have a greater life expectancy?

- How well do you think you were able to consider the arguments in the two short articles and decide whether it is better to invest in health or education to improve life expectancy?

Selecting actions to address an issue

Skills focus
✓ Analysis

Learning focus
- Suggest and compare actions to address an issue.
- Justify actions in terms of their ability to make a positive difference.

Big question: If you were running a country, how could you increase people's life expectancy?

Getting started

1

a) Working on your own, come up with three ways to increase people's life expectancy.

b) Share your ideas with a partner. Between you, agree on the best three.

c) Now, join with another pair and share your ideas. Together, agree on your best three ideas.

d) What evidence would you need to decide which of your group's best three ideas have the greatest chance of success?

Exploring

There are lots of things you could try to change to help people in your country live longer.

2 Read through the following information about the 14 most significant causes of low life expectancy. If there are any ideas you are not clear about, discuss them as a group and ask your teacher for an explanation.

Vocabulary

exposed to: to be placed at risk of something – here, low temperatures

social isolation: having little or no contact with people

social interactions: when people communicate with each other or spend time together

obesity: when a person becomes extremely overweight, usually from eating large quantities of high-calorie foods

diabetes: a medical condition that causes the blood sugar level to get too high

addictive substance: something that people can develop an addiction to

genetic inheritance: traits, such as height and hair colour, passed onto us by our parents through our genes

social security: government assistance, such as funding, provided to people who are unemployed, on low incomes or who are unable to work

---

1 *Poverty*: People who are poor are less likely to be able to access medical treatment, education and healthy food, so they tend to have lower life expectancies.

2 *Homelessness*: Homeless people are less likely to be able to afford healthy food or drinks, and if they sleep outdoors, they may be **exposed** to very low temperatures and a greater risk of violence.

3 *Social isolation*: People who have more **social interactions** tend to live longer, possibly because they are more active and enjoy life more, so have more to live for.

---

4 *Lack of education*: People with a better education tend to live longer, as they are more able to recognise and avoid dangers. They are also more able to access higher paid jobs and information on healthy nutrition and lifestyle.

5 *Fast food*: Fast food tends to be high in salt, sugar and unhealthy fats, and eating too much of it may lead to **obesity**, **diabetes** or other health conditions that shorten life expectancy.

6 *Tobacco and other addictive substances*: Tobacco is one example of an **addictive substance**. Smoking increases the risk of lung cancer, heart disease and other serious life-threatening conditions. All addictive substances increase the risk of physical and mental health problems, and early death.

7 *Genetic inheritance*: People inherit certain characteristics from their parents, and this **genetic inheritance** may affect how long a person is likely to live. For example, if a person's grandparents and parents enjoyed good health into very old age, they will be more likely to do so too.

8 *Stress*: Stress can arise from work or other life circumstances such as poverty, social injustice and poor housing. Long-term stress can lead to health problems such as heart disease and strokes.

9 *Lack of exercise*: Doing little or no physical activity can reduce life expectancy. People with a sedentary lifestyle, where a person sits down a lot of the time, are more likely to put on weight or develop heart problems.

10 *Lack of access to healthcare*: If people need to pay for healthcare, they usually do so through health insurance. If insurance is not available or people cannot afford health insurance, they may not seek help for treatable conditions and their life expectancy may be reduced.

11 *Lack of social security*: **Social security** programmes vary from country to country, but generally they provide an income or facilities if you become incapable of supporting yourself. Such programmes reduce homelessness and improve healthcare, so increasing life expectancy.

Continued on the next page

Low quality of public infrastructure: Countries vary in terms of services such as public transport and medical services. If the quality of **infrastructure** is low, it may be harder for people to access healthcare and education, so reducing life expectancy.

 Diseases: Diseases are more widespread in some areas than in others. If you live in a place where there is more disease, this may reduce life expectancy.

 Parenting: If children are treated with respect, they are more likely to take care of themselves. Also, if parents show their children how to make good decisions, they are likely to live longer, healthier lives.

There are a lot of ideas here for how to increase people's life expectancy. You now need to decide which ideas to prioritise: which are likely to have the most positive impact?

3 Working as a group, sort the 14 most significant causes of low life expectancy into the three groups shown in the table. You need to be prepared to justify your decisions.

a) Factors you think are essential	
b) Factors you think are important but not essential	
c) Factors you think are less important	

4 Compare your table with that of another group. Do you agree about the essentials? Listen to each other's ideas and explore the reasons for your decisions.

Developing

When deciding on actions to be carried out, it is important to consider who will be responsible for **implementing** them. Some factors relating to life expectancy may be down to individual or family actions, whereas others may require actions from the community, government or other outside agencies, such as charities.

Vocabulary

infrastructure: the physical structures, such as roads, transport, power supplies and buildings, needed for a society to function

implement: to put a plan into action

For example, consider these viewpoints on food and nutrition:

> Food is down to the individual and families – it's their choice what they eat.

> Some people may not have access to certain types of food, know how to prepare them or be able to afford them.

5 Working as a group, sort the 14 causes of low life expectancy into the three groups shown in the table.

a) Factors down to individuals and families	
b) Factors requiring community, government or other outside agencies	
c) Factors requiring action from a mixture of both	

Final task

6 Your group has been asked to recommend to the government three ways in which life expectancy can be increased. You will present your recommendations on a poster.

On your poster:

a) Identify the three causes that you think will have the greatest impact.

b) Justify each decision, explaining why it will make a difference.

c) Make it clear who will be responsible for implementing any changes.

d) Explain how it will become clear that these strategies are starting to take effect. For example what changes would you expect to see? How could these changes be monitored?

❷ REFLECTION POINT

Think about how you worked with your group.

- How did you decide which actions to recommend? What process did you use to sort through the different ideas?

- How did you try to persuade others of your ideas?

- How were you influenced by others?

Exploring predictions about the future

Big question: Will yours be the first generation to live to be 100?

Getting started

How likely is it that you will live to be 100 years old? It's an interesting question and, of course, some people do live to be **centenarians**. It is not common, though.

1. If you want to live to 100:
   a) How could you find out how likely this was?
   b) What actions could you take to make living to 100 more likely?

Vocabulary

centenarian: a person who is 100 years or older

Exploring

The chart shows life expectancy in a wide range of countries. It gives the figure in 1970 (the lower white dot) and the figure in 2019 (the higher red dot with number).

Life expectancy at birth, 1970 and 2019

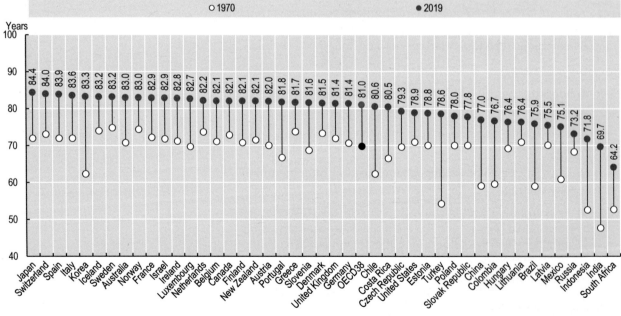

Figure 3.5.1: Life expectancy at birth, 1970 and 2019.
Source: *Health at a Glance 2021: OECD Indicators*, © OECD iLibrary.

2. Study the chart and suggest:
   a) how life expectancy has changed in all these countries
   b) how these changes vary from one country to another.

Let's explore what this might look like in the future. The period from 1970 to 2019 covers 49 years. Let's assume that life expectancy increases by the same amount over the next 49 years, which would take us to 2058. Look again at the graph on page 52 and the increase in life expectancies shown. If that was repeated again, some of those countries would achieve a life expectancy of 100.

3 **a)** The graph on page 52 shows no country as having reached 100 by 2019, yet there are many instances of people living to over 100. Does this mean the graph is wrong?

b) If the increase in life expectancy was repeated over the next 49 years, which countries would have reached 100?

c) What is the major assumption that is being made in this reasoning?

d) How reasonable an assumption do you think this is?

Developing

What will the trend in life expectancy be in the future? There are different points of view on this. In the article 'What happens when we all live to 100?', Andrew Scott suggests that there are three different expert views regarding the future of longevity.

4 Read through the explanation of the three expert views Andrew Scott discusses in his article. For each view, consider how **persuasive** it is. What do you consider the strengths and weaknesses of each argument? Working on your own, make notes on each of these expert views.

Expert view number 1

There is one group of experts that Scott calls the 'levellers'. They argue that the changes that caused the big increases in life expectancy, such as lower infant mortality rates, have had as much impact as they can. Diseases common in wealthy nations such as obesity and cancer are now having a greater impact, and so life expectancy will not continue to improve.

Expert view number 2

Scott calls the second group of experts the 'extrapolators'. They argue that life expectancy will continue to improve, and point out that survival rates for 70-, 80- and 90-year-olds are going up. The rate of increase may be small, but longevity will continue to rise.

Expert view number 3

There is a third group of experts whom Scott calls the 'accelerators'. They argue that there will be an increase in how quickly life expectancy grows. One of the key reasons offered is that people are far better informed about best practice in living long and healthy lives. Most people today understand about good nutrition and hygiene, and how to avoid serious diseases. It is also argued that acting on this knowledge along with health programmes such as exercise and relaxation will enable us to live long enough to benefit from exciting advances in genetics and nanotechnology.

Vocabulary

persuasive: convincing, able to persuade you of the validity of their viewpoint

extrapolate: to predict the future by assuming that current trends will continue in the same way

What do you think will happen to life expectancy over your lifetime, and why do you think that? Do you expect to live longer than your parents – and will your children live longer than you?

When making decisions about these trends, you can look at various types of evidence. For example:

- You might consider how diseases such as measles – which used to kill large numbers of children – are now largely controlled by vaccination.

- You could look at evidence to support the view that more people globally know how to live healthier lives through better nutrition and exercise.

- You could consider evidence to show the impact of new technologies on longevity.

Final task

5 Work in a group to design a poster that shows what you believe to be the most likely scenario for the future of human longevity. Refer to the 'Checklist for success' to help you.

Checklist for success
....

✔ Tell people how you think life expectancy will change in the future.

✔ Explain the reasons for your decisions.

✔ Include evidence from more than one source.

✔ Give clear details about your sources of information.

✔ Lay out the poster clearly for others to read and understand.

✔ Include contributions from all group members.

❷ REFLECTION POINT

This topic is a good example of an area in which evidence can be used to support different conclusions.

- When you were looking at the evidence, how did you decide what to be influenced by? What made you think 'This tells me what is likely to happen in the future'?

- What evidence influenced other students in your class? Was everyone persuaded by the same evidence? How and why did viewpoints differ?

Applying what you have learned

Skills focus
✓ Analysis
✓ Evaluation
Learning focus
• Explore how evidence should be used in decision making.
• Justify actions designed to address a national issue.

Your task

Your group will prepare a presentation in which you select and justify a project to improve the health and life expectancy of people in your country, providing evidence for your choice.

Approaching the task

1. Think back over the ideas you have explored in this topic. You might find it useful to refer to some of the evidence you studied.

2. Now imagine you are the leader of a relatively poor country. A deposit of valuable minerals has just been discovered and the income generated will enable you to fund one of the following three projects:

   • Several properly equipped and staffed hospitals to be located throughout the country.

   • The replacement of sub-standard housing with better accommodation.

   • A health education programme with experts visiting schools and community groups to teach them about health and disease.

   You are committed to improving the health and life expectancy of your people. Your advisers tell you that all three of these programmes will make a positive difference, but you can only select one of them. You need to decide which project you will adopt.

3 Working as a group, discuss each of the three proposals. Consider the evidence you would need to decide which proposal will be the best way of improving the health and life expectancy of people in your country. You might do this using ideas and evidence from:

- sources in this chapter
- other sources you are familiar with
- further research, for example using the internet.

If people in the group have different views, it is important that you can arrive at a final decision.

4 Once your group has decided on the proposal you think will have the greatest positive impact, list the reasons why you think this.

5 Now, prepare a presentation to give to the rest of the class based on your selected idea. Your presentation should include:

- a clear indication of the action you are recommending
- why you think this will be the most successful one
- reasons why you didn't select the other alternatives
- details of evidence you think supports your case.

Read through the 'Checklist for success' for advice on giving a successful presentation.

Checklist for success

✔ Rehearse your presentation to help you get the timing right.

✔ Make sure the points you make are spoken clearly.

✔ Don't read from your notes – it is better to use them as speaking prompts.

✔ Ensure everyone from the group is involved in giving the presentation.

What is your teacher looking for?

Your teacher is looking to see if you can explain and justify your decisions using evidence. This enables other people to see how strong your argument is.

Reflecting on your progress

Look at the 'Check your progress' on the next page and independently assess your learning. Then, with a partner, discuss:

- any new skills you have learned
- what you need to improve
- how the process has helped you to develop your thinking about this issue.

Check your progress

Beginning	Developing	Going beyond
• I can look at evidence and suggest what it shows. • I can consider arguments that have been put forward and suggest how convincing they are. • I can recognise the usefulness of different actions that might be taken to address an issue.	• I can analyse evidence including numerical data and offer a conclusion based on this. • I can evaluate arguments and recognise their strengths and limitations. • I can recognise and compare the different actions that might be taken to address an issue.	• I can develop conclusions based on evidence and suggest how well the evidence supports them, recognising that other conclusions are possible. • I can evaluate how robust an argument is in terms of its supporting evidence. • I can compare different actions to address an issue and justify the selection of some actions over others.

Next steps

- Think of something that has been built, changed or developed in the area where you live. It could be, for example, a new road being built, a different type of medical treatment being offered or a new training course being provided. What evidence do you think was used to decide whether it should go ahead?

- See if you can find out about a development in the area where you live that caused some debate or controversy. It might have been a new business opening or a bus service being withdrawn. Try to find out how it was resolved. What solutions were offered and what was the final outcome?

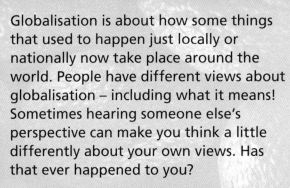

Reflecting on issues
Globalisation

4

Globalisation is about how some things that used to happen just locally or nationally now take place around the world. People have different views about globalisation – including what it means! Sometimes hearing someone else's perspective can make you think a little differently about your own views. Has that ever happened to you?

In this chapter, you will be exploring different perspectives about 'Globalisation'. Because globalisation is such a big topic, you will be looking at just one part of it: choices about food. The issues you will be considering include:

- **What does globalisation mean to you?**

- **What do you think about McDonald's?**

- **What are the causes and consequences of the 'green gold' avocado rush?**

- **What are some of the other consequences of globalisation?**

- **What might make you change your mind about important issues?**

You will be developing a range of analysis and reflection skills:

4.1 Identifying ideas from different perspectives

4.2 Explaining how data are used to back up a perspective

4.3 Explaining causes of a local or global issue and consequences on others

4.4 Reflecting on what makes you change your mind about issues

4.5 Applying what you have learned.

Your final task will be to work in a group to design a school lunch menu that reflects globalisation and food issues that are important to you, including an explanation of why those issues are important.

Identifying ideas from different perspectives

Skills focus
✓ Analysis
✓ Reflection
Learning focus
• Understand what is meant by different perspectives.
• Identify ideas and evidence from sources.

Big question: What does globalisation mean to you?

Getting started

What is a **perspective**? It means a person's 'point of view' and also a person's attitude towards something developed from and supported by evidence.

Do you have the same perspective as the person you are sitting next to about these questions? Let's find out!

🔑 **Key terms**

perspective: a viewpoint on an issue based on evidence and reasoning

1. Work with a partner to ask and answer these questions. Be respectful of each other's opinions.

   a) What is the best topping for pizza?

   b) Which sport is the most fun to watch on TV?

   c) Which school subject is the most useful to study?

   d) How old should children be before they get a mobile phone?

2. These three perspective questions are harder to answer. Why do you think that is? You could discuss this as a class.

   a) Should **single-use plastic** products be made illegal?

   b) Is it wrong to eat meat?

   c) Is it okay to take fashion ideas from cultures other than your own?

Vocabulary

single-use plastic: products made from plastic that are designed to be used just once and then thrown away

Exploring

Globalisation is the topic for this chapter. People have different perspectives about what globalisation is.

Globalisation is about making money. When it becomes easier for countries to trade with each other, that's globalisation.

Globalisation is about people. When people in different countries can communicate with each other in real time and share ideas, that's globalisation.

Globalisation is about culture. When a country's culture is influenced by culture from other countries, that's globalisation.

What does globalisation mean to you?

Globalisation is nothing new – countries in Asia and Europe were trading with each other along the Silk Road for over a thousand years!

Globalisation only became important when people, money and information started to move around the world rapidly.

Identifying ideas from different sources of information is important for developing your analysis skills.

3 a) Work with a partner to put the ideas in these five quotations into your own words.

b) Then use some or all of the ideas to put together your own statement about what globalisation means to you. Here are some ideas for getting started:

☐ 'Globalisation is a big concept. Here are the three most important things to know…'

☐ 'Let's use some examples to show you what globalisation means…'

☐ 'Speaking from personal experience, globalisation…'

> 🔑 **Key terms**
>
> **globalisation**: when what was local and national becomes global because of increasing connections around the world; for example, pizza was once local (Naples, Italy) and is now global

Developing

In Chapter 3, you began developing your analysis skills: identifying ideas and getting **evidence** from sources. Let's recap those skills now with two sources about food – and globalisation. These will help you explore different perspectives about globalisation.

About Me   Contact   Blog   Photo Albums ▼   🔍

🏠 Anton's travel blog

Today's topic: Eating fast food while abroad?

OK, so a few people have asked my advice about fast food when you're travelling. My view is that it is 100 per cent part of the travelling experience to try local food. Yes, fast food is convenient and sometimes it is the only thing available; like when you arrive in a city late. But even then, I would try to eat local fast food, rather than go to the big Western fast-food restaurants. I don't want to judge other travellers – but really, guys! No Big Macs!

For me, travelling is about getting those authentic experiences. Already, so many places around the world seem the same, with the same shops, the same fashions and the same food, served by the same big Western fast-food chains. My take on this: we are losing so much traditional culture. *Vive la différence!*

Hello! My name is Anton: I'm 22, I'm from Canada and for the last year I've been travelling in Europe and Asia.

4. Answer these questions about Anton's travel blog.

   a) What is Anton arguing for here?

   b) List the reasons he gives to back up his argument.

   c) Make a link between Anton's perspective and globalisation.

5 Have a group discussion to explore these questions:

a) What dish or dishes do you consider to be your national food?

b) Why do you think that countries have national dishes?

Final task

6 Think of some questions about this article for a partner to answer. Your questions should:

a) Test whether your partner can identify the main ideas in the article.

b) Ask them to provide evidence to support their answer to question **a**.

c) Ask them to say how the article is linked to globalisation.

d) Ask about their own perspective on the article.

> **Vocabulary**
>
> **pescado frito**: (Spanish) fried fish – a traditional dish from the southern coast of Spain and Portugal

How 'national' are national dishes?

As British as – *pescado frito*?

Part of what makes up a nation's self-image is its national dish. For Jamaica, it might be ackee and saltfish, for Greece – moussaka, and what could be more Irish than Irish stew? We think of these national dishes as 'rooted in the soil' of their nation.

However, the origins of some national dishes suggest a more complicated history. For example, Jewish people forced to leave their homes in Spain and Portugal brought their traditional dish of **pescado frito** – fried fish – to Britain, and that's how we have British fish and chips.

Likewise, 'as American as apple pie' is a well-known saying about another national symbol. However, apples were not native to America: they were brought to the continent by Europeans, while the spices of cinnamon and nutmeg in the pies came from Asia. And the idea of apple pie as being a national dish only began in the 20th century.

So, foods that we might think of as national can sometimes have surprisingly international histories. Globalisation is much older than we might think!

❓ REFLECTION POINT

Working on your own, reflect on how you feel about globalisation now. Are your feelings positive, negative or somewhere in between? Write down your reflection.

Explaining how data are used to back up a perspective

Skills focus
✓ Analysis
Learning focus
• Consider how data are used to support a perspective.
• Reflect on your own views.

Big question: McDonald's – are you loving it?

Getting started

In this unit, you will explore how data are used to back up a perspective and how they are presented so as to make them more convincing. You can learn to spot when data are being used in this way.

A survey asked 100 people what their favourite pizza toppings were. The results were made into this chart.

1 Work with a partner to answer these questions using the chart.

   a) Which topping was the most popular? How do you know?

   b) Which topping was the least popular? How do you know?

   c) Do you think it is a good idea to make a chart about pizza look like a pizza? Why?

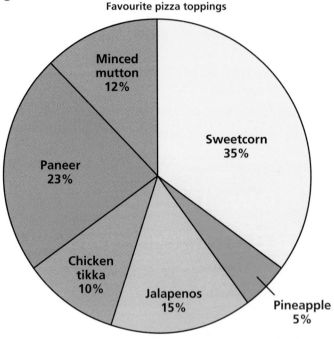

Favourite pizza toppings

- Minced mutton 12%
- Sweetcorn 35%
- Paneer 23%
- Chicken tikka 10%
- Jalapenos 15%
- Pineapple 5%

Figure 4.2.1: Favourite toppings for pizza.

Exploring

There are 38 000 McDonald's restaurants around the world in 119 countries, and 68 million people eat food from McDonald's every day. McDonald's is sometimes called an **icon** of globalisation. There is even a term for this: 'McDonaldization'!

2 Read the text on 'The McDonald's story' on the next page. Which of these statements do you think is the best description of the text's perspective on McDonald's?

   a) The text praises McDonald's and seems proud of the company's success.

   b) The text is a **neutral** account of the facts about McDonald's.

   c) The text is critical of McDonald's.

   d) The text only includes positive information about McDonald's.

Use quotations from the text to back up your answer.

Vocabulary

icon: something widely admired and seen as having great influence

neutral: neither positive nor negative

drive-in customers: customers who purchase a product (such as a meal) without leaving their car

customer service: the assistance provided by a company to the people who buy its products or services

global distribution: how something is spread out across the world

The McDonald's story

The company began in 1948, set up by two brothers: Dick and Mac MacDonald. They developed a fast-food system for making burgers that served **drive-in customers** cheap food (burgers were 15 US cents) very quickly. A businessman called Ray Kroc bought the brothers' company in 1961 for $2.7 million. In ten years, there were over 1000 McDonald's restaurants. Kroc made sure every McDonald's restaurant produced its food in the same way, so it always tasted the same. He found ways to keep McDonald's food very affordable and insisted that **customer service** must always be both very fast and excellent. In 1967, the first McDonald's outside the USA opened in Canada, followed in the same year by one in Costa Rica. By the 1990s, the company reported that it was opening a new restaurant in the world every three hours.

Look at the map showing the number of McDonald's restaurants per person per region in 2018. This type of map is called a **cartogram**. The more McDonald's restaurants a region has, the bigger that region appears on the map. The colours on this map indicate world regions: green for Africa, purple for Europe, and so on.

McDonald's restaurants per person per region, 2018

Figure 4.2.2: A cartogram showing the number of McDonald's restaurants per person per region in 2018.
Source: Based on data from Worldmapper. Map redrawn by Collins Bartholomew.

3 Discuss these questions with a partner and record your thoughts:

a) What does the map tell you about the **global distribution** of McDonald's restaurants?

b) Do you think the way the map presents this information is effective? Why?

c) What perspective do you get from this map about the distribution of McDonald's restaurants? For example, do you think it is making a link between fast food and people's health? What does it suggest about McDonald's as a 'global' company?

> 🔑 **Key terms**
>
> **cartogram**: some maps use colours or shading or icons to show data; a cartogram changes the size and shape of countries or regions to do this

Developing

Globalisation brings big changes. Large **corporations** have become very successful by moving into many different countries. This creates jobs, but it also means more competition for local businesses. It brings new choices for customers, but it also can bring cultural changes.

4 What do you think is meant by the term 'cultural changes'?

As the cartogram on page 65 shows, many regions do not have McDonald's restaurants. These are mostly the poorer areas of the world. McDonald's would not make enough **profit** operating in these regions.

However, there are around eight countries in the world that do not *allow* McDonald's restaurants to open there. The table below has information about four of them.

Country	Since when?	Reason why
Bermuda	1977	To preserve Bermuda's traditions and culture
Iran	1979	Iran and the USA are political enemies
Bolivia	2002	Opposition to big Western corporations and Western **consumer culture**
Montenegro	2003	To protect local restaurants from competition

Table 4.2.3: Four countries that do not allow McDonald's restaurants.

Iceland's last McDonald's closed in 2009. It became too expensive to **import** all the ingredients.

5 Working with a partner, use the information about McDonald's in the table to start creating a list of problems with globalisation. You could put your list into categories, such as:

- Economic (to do with money)
- Political (to do with relationships between countries)
- Cultural (for example, to do with traditions)
- Social (for example, to do with health)
- Environmental.

Record your answers in a table like the one below. Leave the column for positive things blank for now.

	Problems with globalisation	Positive things about globalisation
Economic		
Political		
Cultural		
Social		
Environmental		

Vocabulary

corporation: a large company, often made from grouping together smaller companies

profit: the money a company makes from selling its goods and services after it has paid for all its costs (such as labour, production, distribution)

consumer culture: a culture based on the idea that buying new things is very desirable

import: to buy products or services from another country

Hamilton in Bermuda: no McDonald's allowed.

6 **a)** Research task. Find the answers to two (or more) of these questions online:

    i) What are two things that McDonald's is doing to help reduce its environmental impacts?

    ii) How many people work in McDonald's restaurants around the world?

    iii) What action is McDonald's taking against discrimination and harassment?

    iv) How is McDonald's helping young people to improve their job chances?

b) What does your research tell you about the positives of 'McDonaldization'?

c) Use your ideas to help you develop a list of positives of globalisation. Record your ideas in the 'Positive things about globalisation' column of the table on page 66.

Final task

7 Imagine McDonald's wants to open a new restaurant in your local area. Form three teams:

- a group in favour of the proposal
- a group against the proposal
- a group of elected councillors who need to make a planning decision.

Each side is allowed two speakers to present their case, and the planning committee needs to decide.

❓ REFLECTION POINT

Working on your own, record your perspective on the positives and negatives of globalisation.

Then, compare your reflection with the one you completed for Unit 4.1. Is your thinking on globalisation the same as before, or has it changed at all?

Explaining causes of a local or global issue and consequences on others

Big question: Why are avocados called 'green gold'?

Getting started

1 Look at this diagram, which shows some **causes** and **consequences** of an action.

Cause	Event	Consequence
Ram needed money to buy data for his phone.	I got a job!	Ram has money to buy data for his phone.

Cause		Consequence
Football practice changed to Thursday night. That meant Ram had free time on Saturday.		Ram is very tired on Saturday night and goes to bed early.

Cause	Event	Consequence
Ram saw an **advert** from a fast-food restaurant in his town. The restaurant was looking for workers.	Ram got a job at the fast-food restaurant. He works on Saturday.	Ram has made new friends at work.

a) What were the three causes (or reasons) why Ram got a job at a local fast-food restaurant?

b) What were the three consequences (or effects) of Ram getting a job?

c) Discuss an event with causes and consequences with a partner. Draw a diagram like the one about Ram to show how the causes led to the event, and the consequences followed from the event.

> 🔑 **Key terms**
>
> **cause**: something that makes something else happen; the reason why something happened
>
> **consequence**: the effect or effects something has; what happened because of something

2 Read the following article from a website about globalisation.

a) What is the author talking about when she uses the term 'green gold rush'? Discuss this with a partner. (Hint: think about the phrase 'gold rush' first.)

b) What causes of the 'green gold rush' can you identify from the text? Make a note of them.

c) What consequences of the 'green gold rush' can you find? Note those, too. Can you divide them into local and global consequences?

d) After you have discussed the causes and consequences as a class, draw a causes and consequences diagram like the one featuring Ram to record your findings.

Vocabulary

export: to send goods abroad to be sold

aquifer: underground rock layers that contain water

pesticide: chemical that kills insects or other organisms in order to help crops grow

The avocado 'green gold rush': is it sustainable?

Today, 5 billion kg of avocados are eaten around the world every year. Half of these avocados are grown in Mexico, but before 1994, Mexico could not sell its avocados to the USA. Then, a trade deal between the USA, Canada and Mexico was agreed. Sales of Mexican avocados soared! Unlike in the USA, Mexican farmers can grow avocados all year round. Also, avocados from Mexico are affordable.

Mexico earns $2.8 billion every year from the **export** of avocados. That's why Mexican farmers talk about the 'green gold rush' – avocado farming is very profitable. The minimum wage in Mexico is $5 a day, but avocado plantation workers earn around $60 a day.

Unfortunately, not all the impacts of the 'green gold rush' have been positive. It takes over 220 litres of water to grow one avocado. In Mexico, this water comes from underground **aquifers** that can take hundreds of years to fill. Also, in order to have more land to grow avocados on, farmers in Mexico have cut down forests. Furthermore, avocado plantations use **pesticides** that damage bees, and carbon emissions to transport avocados around the world are very high.

In 2010, China's imports of avocados were worth just $4000. Five years later, China's avocado imports were worth $24 million. This is good news for Mexico's avocado farmers – but is it sustainable for Mexico's environment and for the world?

GreenGrandma: Where can I buy avocados that don't have bad impacts on the environment?

Purple Biscuit: Is avocado on toast actually healthy? Looks too green lol

❓ REFLECTION POINT

What comment or comments would you post if you had read this article online?

Developing

One consequence of globalisation is that consumers can eat food from all round the world. This has benefits but also causes problems.

3 Study these images and work with others to decide what some of the positive and negative consequences of food globalisation might be.

Here are some terms to use in your discussion:

> food waste   seasonal produce   deforestation   consumer choice   food miles

4 Read this article from a science magazine. What does this article say about the consequences of our diet for climate change? Discuss this with a partner.

Food production emissions make up more than a third of global total

by Krista Charles

Food production contributes around 37 per cent of global **greenhouse gas (GHG) emissions**, showing the huge impact that our diets have on climate change. What's more, animal-based foods produce roughly twice the emissions of plant-based ones. […]

According to [research] estimates, global food production contributes about 17.3 billion metric tonnes of carbon dioxide equivalent per year, almost 19 times the amount from the **commercial aviation** industry. Of these emissions, 57 per cent were related to the production of animal-based foods and plant-based food production accounted for 29 per cent. The remaining emissions came from agricultural land being converted from non-food crops like cotton to food production.

Source: *New Scientist*, 13 September 2021.

> **Vocabulary**
>
> **greenhouse gas (GHG) emissions**: gas(es) that trap heat in the atmosphere, causing it to warm; GHGs include, for example, carbon dioxide and methane
>
> **commercial aviation**: aircraft that transport people and goods for business purposes

5 Look at the graphic, which compares the greenhouse gas (GHG) emissions of different types of diet in the USA. The figures show greenhouse gas emissions in tonnes.

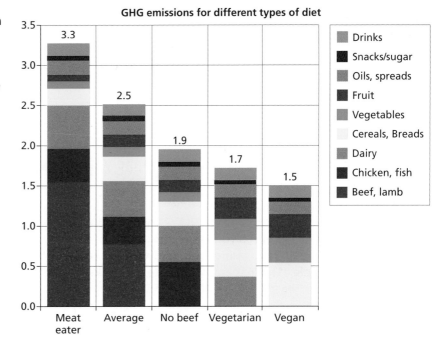

GHG emissions for different types of diet

Legend:
- Drinks
- Snacks/sugar
- Oils, spreads
- Fruit
- Vegetables
- Cereals, Breads
- Dairy
- Chicken, fish
- Beef, lamb

Values: Meat eater 3.3, Average 2.5, No beef 1.9, Vegetarian 1.7, Vegan 1.5

a) Which diet has the highest GHG emissions and which the lowest?

b) What type of meat produces the most GHGs?

c) What is the difference between vegetarian and vegan?

Figure 4.3.1: Greenhouse gas emissions in tonnes per person for different types of diet.
Source: Shrink That Footprint

Final task

6 Look at the two food items: avocado toast and lamb kebab.

- The avocados have been imported to your country by plane from a farm 15 000 km away.

- The meat from the kebab comes from a local farm in your country, 15 km away.

In groups, decide:

a) What are the consequences of choosing these foods? For example, you could mention how avocado production in Mexico has increased deforestation.

b) Which of these two foods has the worst environmental consequences and why?

Look back over the work you've done so far in this unit to help you. Present your thinking to the rest of the class. Read through the 'Checklist for success' to help you.

Checklist for success

✔ Introduce your ideas clearly and simply.

✔ Speak clearly when it is your turn.

✔ Give reasons for your suggestions.

✔ Avoid reading word for word from your notes; instead, use speaking prompts.

✔ End by asking the class if they have any questions.

? REFLECTION POINT

Does it matter what we eat? Would you make any changes to what you eat as a result of your investigations into food and globalisation? Record your thoughts about this question, working on your own.

Reflecting on what makes you change your mind about issues

Big question: What might make you change your mind?

Getting started

1 What does it feel like when you really think about something? Write a **simile** about the feelings you get when you're thinking hard. For example, 'Thinking feels like little fireworks popping' or 'When I think really hard, it's like pushing a heavy sack over a high wall.'

As you saw in Chapter 1, **reflection** is a specific kind of thinking. It is important for learning and making progress. When you reflect on something, you think about how you did it and why you did it. You ask yourself questions about what you might do differently next time, and about what has changed in the way you think.

Exploring

Around the world, organisations work hard to find out what we think about things. This can be for different reasons: from companies wanting to sell us products to politicians wanting us to vote for them.

2 Write down your own answers to the following questions.

> **Vocabulary**
>
> **simile**: a comparison of two different things using the words 'like' or 'as'

> 🔑 **Key terms**
>
> **reflection**: thinking carefully about what you do (or have done) and how you do it in a way that helps you make progress

A Would you rather be able to travel backwards in time or forwards in time?			
☐ Backwards in time	☐ Forwards in time	☐ Neither	☐ Don't know

B Which of the following would you rather have named after you?		
☐ An island	☐ A shopping mall	☐ A baby

C Which superpower would you most like to have?		
☐ Invisibility	☐ Flying	☐ Super strength

3 **a)** Discuss your answers to the survey as a group. Share the answers you gave, and the reasons why (unless you would rather keep them to yourself).

b) Then, reflect individually on how you felt when:

- most people gave the same answer as you (if this happened)

- most people gave a different answer to you (if this happened).

c) Did the answers (and reasons) from other people in the group make you change your mind about your own answer?

4 Read the following information about three celebrities. As you read it, think about how it makes you feel.

Are the facts provided about the three celebrities positive or negative in your view?

Footballer Neymar Jr has given over US$6 million to a children's charity in São Paulo, Brazil.

In 2021, singer and songwriter Nicki Minaj shared rumours that Covid-19 vaccines might be harmful with her 21 million followers on Twitter.

Hollywood actor Zac Efron is a vegan.

5 Read this further information about Nicki Minaj:

Nicki Minaj donates money to a village in India to improve water supplies and computer access, and in 2020 she funded the construction of a recreation centre in Trinidad and paid $25,000 to a girls' school.

Did this new information make you change your view of Nicki Minaj?

6 Now pick one of these three questions to discuss with a partner:

a) Are we sometimes too quick to make up our minds about people?

b) Are we more interested in negative information about people than positive information?

c) Is being famous harder for women than men?

Developing

7 **a)** What are you going to eat for lunch today (or what have you already eaten)?

b) Compare your choice with the rest of your class. You could work in groups to present the data as a graph, like the one below.

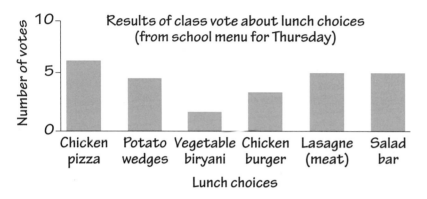

Results of class vote about lunch choices
(from school menu for Thursday)

Today's menu

Veg curry
Gulab jamun
Spinach rice
Paneer curry
Plain rice
Tomato dal
Chapati
Kheera raita
Yoghurt

Tasty, nutritious food!

8 Next, do some analysis of the results, looking at greenhouse gas (GHG) emissions.

a) Which of the choices were meat-based, which were veggie (vegetarian), and which were vegan? You could record your results in a chart like this:

Meal	Beef/lamb	Chicken/fish/ other meat	Dairy	Vegetables/ fruits	GHG score
Chicken pizza	✗	✓	✓	✓	
Potato wedges	✗	✗	✗	✓	
Vegetable biryani	✗	✗	✓	✓	
Chicken burger	✗	✓	✓	✓	
Lasagne (meat)	✓	✓	✓	✓	
Salad bar	✗	✗	✗	✓	

b) This analysis gives you insights into the GHG emissions of the different meals (look back at page 71). Work out a scoring system for GHG emissions, for example:

Vegan meals (vegetables or fruit, no dairy, no meat)   scores 1

Vegetarian meals (vegetables or fruit, dairy, no meat)   scores 3

Lower GHG meat (includes chicken, fish)   scores 4

Higher GHG meat (includes lamb or beef)   scores 8

(Beef and lamb production is responsible for 50% of GHG emissions globally.)

(There are food emission calculators online that you could use to get detailed results.)

c) Then complete an analysis looking at food culture. For example, what country or world region are the meals originally from? You could use a chart like this to record your analysis:

Meal	Food culture	
Chicken pizza	Italy	
Potato wedges	USA	
Vegetable biryani	India	Pakistan
Chicken burger	USA	
Lasagne (meat)	Italy	
Salad bar	USA	

Final task

9 Continue this analysis for the whole school menu. Is your school menu more international than national, or does it feature more meals from the country you are in? If it is more international than national, which cultures' foods feature most often?

10 Think about these two questions on your own:

a) What consequences do my own food choices have for other people and other places?

b) Has looking at different perspectives about food and globalisation changed how I feel about my food choices?

Make a note of your reflections on these questions.

11 Finally, as a class, repeat the survey of lunch choices – this time for what people intend to eat tomorrow.

a) Analyse the results in your group.

b) Do the results show any changes or not? What conclusions does your group have about this?

❓ REFLECTION POINT
Think about a time when you changed your mind. What was it that made you decide differently?

Applying what you have learned

Skills focus
✓ Reflection

Learning focus
- Explore perspectives.
- Reflect on perspectives.

Your task

Your group will design a school lunch menu that is informed by what you have discovered about globalisation and food. You can design a completely new menu, or you can suggest how your school's menu could be changed and improved.

Approaching the task

Vocabulary

concept map: diagram that shows the connections between ideas and concepts visually

1 The first step is to reflect on the main issues of globalisation and food. You could do this as a **concept map**.

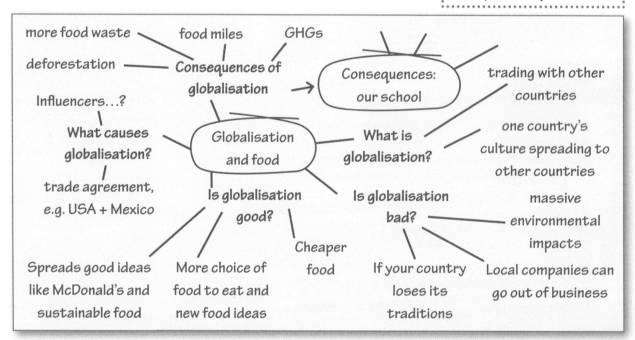

- Everyone can add ideas, or you might want to choose one person to write (a scribe).
- There are no bad ideas at this stage: write them all down.
- Draw lines to show how ideas are connected.

2 Next, focus on the issues of globalisation and food that are important to your group. These will be the ideas you want your school lunch menu to reflect.

What is your teacher looking for?

Your teacher is looking for evidence that all group members are taking part. They might ask you to talk about how you have contributed.

One way to do this is:

- ☐ Step 1: Everyone lists their top three issues.
- ☐ Step 2: Compare the issues as a group.
- ☐ Step 3: Use the issues that got listed the most.

Your top three issues are your project objectives. Record these on a whiteboard or a big piece of paper so that everyone in the team can see them as they work.

3 Now, decide as a group how your top three issues fit with school menu choices. For example:

> More food cultures = include meals from new food cultures (for example, West African countries?)
>
> Reduce deforestation = ensure sustainable food supplies (no palm oil?)
>
> Promote local = include meals that reflect our local food culture, with ingredients from local suppliers

4 Work together as a group to design your school's lunch menu. The finished menu could be completed as an A3 poster. Group members will need to decide who does what. Possible roles could be:

- researchers
- designers
- illustrators/picture researchers
- content checkers
- project manager.

5 As a group, prepare to present your finished menu.
Read through the 'Checklist for success' to help you.

What is your teacher looking for?
....
Your teacher may collect or look at your list of important issues, so make sure your name is on it somewhere. The whole group should be able to explain why your top issues are important.

What is your teacher looking for?
....
Your group should be able to explain who has what role and what the responsibilities of that role are. Be ready to describe how you worked together to solve problems!

Checklist for success
....
- ✔ Make sure you can explain the issues that were important to you for this task.
- ✔ Be able to talk about research and the sources for your ideas and inspirations.
- ✔ Refer back to your project objectives.
- ✔ Explain the choices you have made for your menu.
- ✔ Make sure you ask for feedback.

Reflecting on your progress

Think about how you worked as part of a team. What went well and what could have been improved? What could you work on for the next time you are a team member?

Check your progress

Beginning	Developing	Going beyond
• I can recognise that people think different things about globalisation.	• I can identify some key points from different perspectives about globalisation.	• I can identify perspectives and put together arguments and evidence from a range of sources about globalisation.
• I can say what I think graphical or numerical data show.	• I can find some patterns in graphical or numerical data and say what I think they mean.	• I can explain how graphical or numerical data support an argument or a perspective.
• I can talk about the causes of things I do and what the consequences are for others.	• I can talk about the causes of things that happen in my local area and what the consequences are for others.	• I can talk about the causes of things that happen in my local area and globally, and what the consequences are for others.
• I can talk about what I've learned during an activity and consider how my ideas have changed.	• I can talk about ways that my ideas may have been influenced by new information or the ideas of others.	• I can consider ways that my perspective on an issue may have changed as a result of conducting research or exploring different perspectives.

Next steps

- Talk to people you know about whether food choices have changed over the last few years: for example, are there more vegan choices in local shops, cafés and restaurants?

- Discuss catering with people who provide meals in your school. What perspectives do they have about the challenges of providing food that is affordable, attractive to young people and includes healthy choices.

Communicating your ideas

Values and beliefs

5

When humans work together, they can achieve so much more than when they work alone. The flags in this photo are from the United Nations, an organisation in which countries work together to tackle international problems. However, groupwork is difficult. It involves compromise – giving up a bit of what you might want to achieve to get something the whole group can agree with. It requires good communication skills, especially listening to others.

In this chapter, you will be exploring the topic of 'Values and beliefs'. The issues you will be considering include:

- **What values do we have in common?**
- **Can you teach teamwork?**
- **How can we help each other to improve as a team?**
- **Where is the 'me' in team?**

You will be developing a range of communication, collaboration and reflection skills:

5.1 Listening to ideas and making valuable contributions

5.2 Working effectively as a team

5.3 Presenting information clearly

5.4 Reflecting on the benefits of teamwork

5.5 Applying what you have learned.

Your final task will be to work as a group to tell a story about values and human rights.

Listening to ideas and making valuable contributions

Skills focus
✓ Communication
Learning focus
• Reflect on what is important to you.
• Listen to what other people value.
• Communicate your own views.

Big question: What values do we have in common?

Getting started

 1 Read the definition of **values**.

  a) What values are important to you?

  b) Pick a top three.

> **Vocabulary**
>
> **values**: what is important to you; the principles that guide your life

> Friendliness   Determination   Creativity   Being healthy   Having fun   Learning
> Optimism   Trustworthiness   Independence   Resilience (toughness)   Compassion
> Courage   Commitment   Kindness   Calmness   Loyalty   Honesty   Generosity

The ancient Greek philosopher Aristotle (384–322 BCE) wrote about virtues – what we might call values. In his view, we become the people we want to be by practising the values that are important to us.

2 Do you agree with Aristotle – that you need to practise being the person you want to be?

Exploring

3 Read the text about the creation of the Universal Declaration of Human Rights (UDHR). Then work with a partner to discuss these questions about the text.

  a) What are 'human rights'?

  b) Why did the United Nations want a document about human rights?

  c) Why was the Commission made up of people from different cultural backgrounds?

  d) Which do you think was more important for the Commission to work well: that Commission members could communicate their values clearly, or that members listened carefully to each other?

  e) Do you think it was difficult for the members of the Commission to work together? Explain why or why not.

The United Nations Universal Declaration of Human Rights

In 1946, after the end of the Second World War, work began on the **Universal Declaration** of Human Rights (UDHR), an international document that set out the rights and freedoms of all humans everywhere. People wanted to make sure the atrocities of the war and the **genocide** of persecuted people could never happen again.

The **Commission** on Human Rights started work on the declaration. The Commission had 18 members from different countries and backgrounds, including members from Australia, China, Chile, Lebanon and Canada. The head of the Commission was Eleanor Roosevelt from the USA.

The members of the Commission came from very different cultural backgrounds. These differences were important. They wanted the declaration to be 'universalist', which means true for everyone rather than coming from one particular culture, religion or political system.

Next, the declaration was discussed by the member states of the **United Nations**. On 10 December 1948, 50 member nations of the United Nations agreed the declaration, and eight countries **abstained**.

Eleanor Roosevelt and members of the Commission on Human Rights at a meeting in 1946

Eleanor Roosevelt with a poster of the Universal Declaration of Human Rights.

Vocabulary

Universal Declaration: a statement that applies to everyone

genocide: murdering people because they are from a particular ethnic group or nation with the aim of killing everyone like them

commission: a group of people given a specific job to do by a government or international organisation

United Nations: an international organisation that aims to keep the world peaceful by helping countries sort out their differences by talking rather than fighting

abstained: decided not to vote for or against something

Developing

4 An important skill to develop to help you work together effectively is good listening. Work in a group, with a partner or on your own to try out these activities.

a) Body language is important for good listening. As a group, get into poses to show body language for 'I am not listening' and 'I am listening'. You can exaggerate them to really show what good listening looks like. Practise using 'I am listening' body language when you are listening.

Does this look like good listening?

b) Showing you have listened is important for good listening. After someone has finished their point, give a quick summary of what you've heard. For example, you can say, 'So if I've understood you correctly, you think that…?' Look back at the values you decided were important to you (page 80). With a partner, practise listening: one of you explains your values and the reasons for them, and then the other recaps what they have been told.

c) What other things are important for good listening? Jot down ideas on your own. For example, what about waiting for someone to finish speaking before you start talking? Do you have any ideas for helping to stop people interrupting or talking over others? Share your ideas with your partner.

Language support

Try these useful phrases for showing your response to another person's ideas:

- 'While I see the advantages of that, I wonder if…'

- 'In my opinion…'

- 'One option could be to…'

- 'That's an interesting idea, but have you considered…?'

5 Go back to the values that you decided were important to you (page 80).

a) As a group, decide on a value or values for your group that you all agree is or are important. You could discuss school values for this. Make sure you have listened carefully and respectfully to everyone in the group.

b) Design a **logo** for your group that shows or reflects your shared values.

Final task

6 In your group, research all 30 articles of the UDHR, so that you understand what each one means. (A couple of articles are summarised below.) Your teacher may give you information about the 30 articles or you can find information online.

a) You will need to decide how best to carry out this task in the time available. Make a note of how you did this.

b) Make sure that if anyone in the group has questions about what any of the articles mean, or individual words in the explanations, that these questions are recorded. Work out a way to find the answers you need. Note down the way you did this.

c) As a group, decide which five of the 30 articles are the most important. Find a way to do this fairly, so everyone has a say. Record how you did this.

> **Vocabulary**
>
> **logo**: a symbol or a little design that helps others recognise where something comes from

Article 8 says that human rights should be protected by law.

Article 29 says we have community duties and responsibilities.

> **What is your teacher looking for?**
>
> Your teacher is looking to see if you can explain and justify your decisions using evidence. This enables other people to see how strong your argument is.

> **Study skills**
>
> Look back at 'Applying what you have learned' in Chapter 4 to remind yourself about skills for making group decisions.

> **? REFLECTION POINT**
>
> Think about how you worked as part of a team. What could you do differently next time you do groupwork to improve your teamwork?

Working effectively as a team

Big question: Can you teach teamwork?

Getting started

1 Which jobs do you think need the best teamwork? Are there any jobs that don't need people to work well as a team? Here are some jobs to consider.

| School teacher | Firefighter | Journalist | Software developer |

| Social media influencer | Fashion designer | Fitness trainer |

Exploring

2 Work in a group to try out these two activities.

a) Get knotted! Arrange your group in a circle, holding hands. Two people from the group are not in the circle.

• Those in the circle tangle themselves up – move towards the other side of the circle, go under people's hands, go through their legs if they are standing. Keep holding hands.

• The two who are not in the group now give instructions to untangle the knot.

b) Silent sorting. This activity is carried out in silence – no speaking at all!

The class splits into two groups; each group arranges themselves into a line, facing each other.

One person will tell you all to sort yourselves into a particular order. The rest of you must do this without speaking. Possible orders could be:

- by height (shortest first)
- by birthday (youngest first)
- by middle name (alphabetically).

There will be a check at the end to see if the order is correct.

3 In your group, discuss:

a) Which activity, a or b, was most fun? (You could give each a score.)

b) What did you all find hardest and easiest about the activities?

- Did everyone feel the same or were there differences?
- Did you make any adaptations to the activities, for example with members of your team who have disabilities?

c) What do you think the activities were trying to achieve? They are both teamwork activities, but what teamworking skills was each one focusing on?

d) Teamworking involves **collaboration**. Write a sentence using the term 'collaboration' to show you understand what the term means.

4 What values are involved in good teamwork, do you think? Make a list.

> ## 🔑 Key terms
>
> **collaboration**: working together with others to produce or achieve something

> ## Study skills
>
> Look again at the word cloud from from Question **1b)** on page 80 to help you decide which values are useful for teamwork.

Developing

5 Read the extract on the next page. It is part of an article about teamwork from a business website.

a) What values does the website identify as being important for teamwork?

b) Are there other values that you think are important for teamwork that are not mentioned here?

Five insights for great teamwork

You have recruited the best individuals for your organisation, so why are your teams underperforming? Let's focus your teamwork with these five tips from the top of business management.

A question to start: what is a team? Is a team the same as a group – or is it different? The difference is that a team has a focus. A team is put together to achieve something specific, to get a particular job done. Which leads us to our first **insight**!

Insight #1: Goals

A team is there for a reason. Everyone needs a clear understanding of the team's goals. If people do whatever they want rather than working towards team goals, then there's no team.

Insight #2: Roles

Everyone needs to know their role: what they need to do to meet the team goals. If people aren't sure, the team will struggle. Team members must take responsibility for their role.

Insight #3: Fairness

If only some team members do the work, or get rewarded for the team's achievements, then the team may fail. Work, and praise, needs to be shared out fairly among the team.

Insight #4: Trust

Teams need trust and loyalty: members need to be able to rely on each other. This comes from working together, supporting each other and sharing achievements. Without trust, blame, frustration and infighting can cause a team to fail.

Insight #5: Communication

Teams need a clear focus, with clear roles and responsibilities. Effective communication comes from the top – the leadership role.

With these five insights, you can transform teamwork and start achieving amazing results.

User1287: Please share references for the research that supports these insights.

Vocabulary

insight: a way of understanding something more deeply or accurately

Many organisations spend time and money on team-building activities. This suggests teams don't just happen when you put a group of people together and tell them to achieve a goal.

6 Look at this photo.

a) What do you think the participants have to do for this activity?

b) How do you think this activity would help to build a team? (Think about values.)

Final task

7 Work in a group to research and plan a team-building activity to teach to the rest of the class. Decide how your group will deliver (teach) the activity. You will need to:

a) Remind yourself about internet research skills by looking back at Unit 2.2.

b) Decide on roles for the task. As well as researchers, you may need:

- someone to record the results

- someone to coordinate the research or make sure you finish in time.

c) You will need to think about:

- Does your group need a leader?

- How will you choose which team-building activity is the best one for you to do?

d) Decide as a group how you will teach your chosen activity. Of course, everyone must have a role in teaching. What resources will you need? What other questions will you need answers to?

> **Study skills**
>
> Make sure you use and improve your listening skills so you can work effectively as a team.

❓ REFLECTION POINT

Thinking about the final task, how did you agree as a team about what you were going to do? How could you improve this further next time you work together?

Presenting information clearly

Skills focus
✓ Communication
Learning focus
• Present information.
• Give feedback.

Big question: How can we help each other to improve as a team?

Getting started

1 Student groups each did a presentation, and the rest of the class gave **feedback**. Here is some of the feedback. Read what people had to say, then answer the questions that follow.

> Abi was amazing! She was the best – so glad we're best friends!!!

> One group spoke too quickly, and I couldn't hear everything.

> Group A had really good slides. I liked the pictures because it made the presentation more interesting.

> Group B. That was just embarrassing! Next time you should practise the presentation first. Then you would know who was supposed to say what.

> Everyone was really good at something. It's just really hard to compare you all. So, I guess – great job everyone?

🔑 **Key terms**

feedback: information given about the results of an activity that is intended to improve results next time the activity is done

a) What is good about the feedback? What is not so helpful?

b) Which feedback is best and why?

Exploring

2 Reflect on your own experiences of feedback.

a) How does your school communicate feedback?

b) What do you find useful about feedback on schoolwork?

c) What do you find challenging or not so helpful about it?

Feedback is a key part of sports coaching.

3 Read the checklist for **communicating** effective feedback in Table 1.

a) Working with a partner, give each other effective feedback in one or more of these imaginary scenarios.

b) You could also try to act out examples of feedback being communicated badly!

🔑 Key terms

communicating: exchanging information with others

generalising: making a general rule or statement that is then applied to other cases

Scenarios

- A parent talking to their young child about their messy room.
- A teacher communicating feedback to a student about their homework.
- A manager giving feedback to an employee about their work.

Checklist	Example of good feedback		Example of poor feedback	
✓ Identify the goal	Parent:	We agreed that you would tidy your room on Sundays, didn't we?	Parent:	Your room is a disgrace, Jay! I'm tired of tidying up after you all day.
✓ Be specific	Parent:	If you put the cars into their box and all the plastic bricks into the big container, that will be tidy enough.	Parent:	Your room's not tidy enough, Jay.
			Jay:	How tidy does it have to be?
			Parent:	Tidy means tidy!
✓ Give feedback on actions, not the person	Parent:	Jay, you haven't tidied your room.	Parent:	Jay, your room is a disgrace!
	Jay:	I meant to, but I forgot.	Jay:	Sorry I forgot to tidy it.
	Parent:	Here's your reminder.	Parent:	You always 'forget' things you don't want to do, Jay!
✓ Avoid **generalising**	Parent:	I reminded you to tidy your room. Did you tidy it?	Parent:	Why is your room *always* so messy! You *never* tidy it when I tell you to!
✓ Use statements, not questions	Parent:	Your room is looking much tidier, Jay.	Parent:	Is that what you call tidy, Jay?
✓ Be consistent with other feedback	Parent:	It's Sunday, Jay – room tidying day.	Sister:	Mum and Dad said to tidy your room today, Jay.
	Jay:	Dad said we could play football.	Jay:	But you said we could play football.
	Parent:	Tidying first.	Sister:	Oh yes, I forgot. Let's go to the park.

Developing

In Unit 5.2, your group researched team-building activities and selected an activity to teach to the rest of the class. You will now teach your team-building activity to the other groups, who will then give you feedback. Other groups will also be teaching you a team-building activity, and you will be giving them feedback.

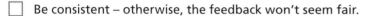

Your group's feedback needs to:

☐ Agree on the goals of the activities. Your feedback can then help groups get closer to those goals.

☐ Be specific, so the groups know what they need to improve.

☐ Be consistent – otherwise, the feedback won't seem fair.

4 As a class, agree what the goals of the team-building activities should be. It will be useful to:

- Break down overall goals into smaller (mini) goals, because it is difficult to give feedback on one big goal, for example 'teach a team-building activity well'. These mini goals could be focused on key skills.

- Be specific about what success in each mini goal looks like. This will help with giving consistent feedback.

- Put the goals into a template for everyone to share and use so everyone can give feedback on the same things and in the same way. An example is given below.

Feedback for group presentations

Group name: _____ Date: _____

Skill	What great looks like	Great	Good	OK	Not good	Bad	What bad looks like	How to improve
Organisation	Very clear structure to presentation						Information all jumbled up, no clear structure	
Visuals	Images were relevant and added interest						Images were distracting and not relevant	
Time	Presentation ran to time (10 mins)						Presentation was over or under time by a lot	
Communication skills	Presenters spoke clearly, without hesitation and at a good pace						Presenters mumbled; weren't sure what to say; spoke much too fast/slow	
Aims	Reasons for the choice of activity were given						No reasons were given for the activity choice	
Content	The content was well-researched and relevant						There was no evidence of research; content was not relevant	

5 Use the feedback template that you have developed as a class to plan and practise teaching your team-building activity. For example, if one of the mini goals is 'Everyone in the group has a role', then make sure everyone has a role.

Final task

6 Deliver your team-building activity to the rest of the class. Read through the presentation skills checklist to help you. Remember to:

*   Give reasons why your group chose your team-building activity – what it is designed to help with.

*   Include references: put on the slides where you found your activity using a clear referencing style. One style of doing this uses this approach:

Surname, Initial. (Date) *Title*. [Online] (Date accessed).
Available from: URL.

For example:

> Das, R. (2022) *How to reference websites*. [Online] 12 May 2022.
> Available from: www.madeupwebsiteforthisexample.com

Checklist for success

Presentation skills

✔ Start with a list of key points.

✔ Have a clear beginning, middle and end.

✔ Don't have too many images, and don't include animations – they are distracting.

✔ Use a font that is easy to read.

✔ Practise your presentation with a timer.

✔ Stick to your script.

✔ Make eye contact.

✔ Try not to read from notes.

✔ Allow time for questions.

7 You will then receive feedback from the other teams. When receiving feedback:

*   Try not to argue back if you don't agree with the points made.

*   Check that you have understood the feedback properly by summarising it, for example by saying, 'So, if I understand you correctly, your point is…'

*   Focus on how the feedback could help you improve (growth mindset).

8 Give feedback to other teams on their activities using your agreed feedback templates.

❓ REFLECTION POINT

As a group, reflect on the feedback that you received for your team-building activity.

Make notes on what you would do to improve your teaching of a team-building activity next time. Be specific.

Reflecting on the benefits of teamwork

Skills focus
✓ Reflection
Learning focus
- Reflect on learning.
- Reflect on working in a group.

Big question: Where is the me in team?

Getting started

1 Read the extracts from Eleanor Roosevelt's 'My Day' newspaper column.

a) What do you understand by the word 'reflect'?

b) What were Eleanor Roosevelt's reflections on her work with the Universal Declaration of Human Rights (UDHR)? What do her reflections say about teamwork and collaboration?

c) How do you think her reflections helped her achieve the goal of the UDHR?

A statue of Eleanor Roosevelt celebrates her role as the first US delegate to the United Nations.

'My Day' by Eleanor Roosevelt, October 15, 1948

At lunch yesterday with some of my Latin-American colleagues I learned something that I must not forget. I had made the suggestion that we might **hasten** our work by **curtailing** the number of speeches and found on the part of one of my colleagues a real objection to the idea that anyone should not be allowed to speak [...] I think that I will remember in the future that it would be better to appeal to one's colleagues to speak briefly but never to suggest that they give up their right to speak [...]

'My Day' by Eleanor Roosevelt, November 23, 1948

Article 23 of the Declaration of Human Rights was discussed and amended [...] I must say I do not like the composition of this article as much as that which was originally drafted. The effort to get in everybody's ideas, I think, resulted in so much detail that [...] I think it is now overloaded and somewhat meaningless [...]

When you work with an international group, you learn that one person's point of view must be [seen as less important than] the will of the majority and so Article 23 passed [...]

> **Vocabulary**
>
> **hasten**: speed up
>
> **curtailing**: reducing

2 This diagram gives a way of thinking about reflection and how it helps learning.

The part of the diagram for 'What?' has two sentences underneath that explain more about what 'What?' means.

a) Write similar sentences to explain what 'So what?' and 'Now what?' mean.

b) Think about how reflection works as you do this.

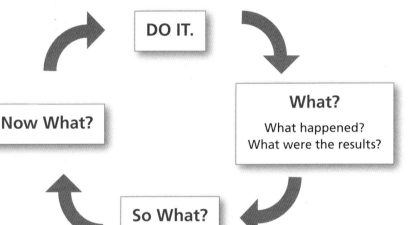

DO IT.

Now What?

What?
What happened?
What were the results?

So What?

3 Here's a piece of reflective writing that uses these same headings. Use the same approach to write a reflection on the team-building activity you completed in Unit 2.3.

What?	I started a new video game. I found its steering system too difficult.
So what?	I got frustrated with the game. I wished I hadn't spent so much money on it.
Now what?	I'm going to watch online videos on how to steer.

4 Teachers use different approaches to help students reflect on their learning. Here are a few for you to try out.

a) Sentence starters to help you get reflecting:

> Today I found out about...
> The question I asked today was...
> I want to find out more about...
> What's next for me is...

b) Ideas to help you switch into reflection mode:

- Draw a quick sketch of what you did and add notes for 'So what?' and 'Now what?'

  - Write or record a 'My Day' column of your own for a week.

5 Think about values that are important to you. For each one, identify the value and then give a reason why reflection helps you practise that value in your life. For example:

> Resilience: what I like about reflection is that I can learn from my mistakes and that makes me be better and stronger each time!

Developing

6 How can we reflect on groupwork? Read the example about the UDHR below. Discuss these questions: Is it fair to judge how well a group worked together:

a) by what the group achieved?

b) by identifying how much work each member of the group did?

Early drafts of the UDHR which the United Nations keeps in its archives.

Reflecting on the UDHR

One way to tell if a group has worked well together is to look at the results the group achieved. However, this won't tell you how well the group worked together, and what could be improved for next time.

For example, the UDHR was put together by a group of 18 people, and all countries of the United Nations were asked to support it. Before the UDHR was finalised, 168 different versions of the declaration were considered in 81 different meetings. That's a *lot* of feedback.

To get a result that everyone could agree with, there had to be **compromise**. The group who put the UDHR together had to listen to feedback, think about ways to include it that did not cause problems for other countries or for the overall aim of the UDHR, make the changes and then present a new draft (version) to another meeting. When countries saw that their feedback had been considered, they were more likely to support the UDHR – even if it had not been possible to fix everything they wanted.

Many organisations have project managers whose job is to help projects meet their goals. A key part of the project manager's role is to hold 'Lessons learned' meetings. These identify:

- what went right

- what went wrong

- what needs to be improved.

Often, the first step of a lessons learned meeting is a survey. The project manager sends this out to each member of the team. The aim is to gather feedback. An example is given on the next page.

> **Vocabulary**
>
> **compromise**: giving up something you want in order to reach an agreement with someone else

7 Imagine you are Eleanor Roosevelt. What feedback might she have given to a survey like this one about the Commission's work producing the UDHR?

Final task

8 Working in a group, create a survey like this one for your team-building teaching activity.

a) Each member of the group should complete it.

b) One member of the group should compile (put together) the results of the survey and chair (lead) a 'Lessons learned' meeting.

c) Before the meeting, decide as a group on rules for the lessons learned discussions. Base these on values. For example:

- Honesty: we should be honest about what went wrong.

- Calmness: no shouting.

- Generosity: we should praise what others did well.

d) Stick to an agenda for the meeting. Make sure one group member takes notes on what was discussed.

Presentation project lessons learned survey

Group name: _____ Your name: _____

Please describe your role in the project:

Please give your honest opinion about the following statements.

For each statement, use the rating scale 1 to 5, where 1 is strongly disagree and 5 is strongly agree, to indicate your response to each statement.

	Statements	1	2	3	4	5
1	Our group had a clear goal that everyone understood					
2	We had all the things we needed to complete the project (e.g., paper, pens, internet access...)					
3	We used our time effectively and were able to complete the project on time					
4	I completely understood what my role was in the project					
5	I was able to make contributions to the project					
6	We worked well together as a group					
7	We were able to achieve our goal					
8	I improved my presentation skills in this project					
9	We used feedback from others to find ways to improve					

10 What went well on this project?

11 What was most challenging about this project?

12 What issues about this project would you like to discuss at the lessons learned meeting?

❓ REFLECTION POINT

What do you think is:

a) good about teamwork?

b) challenging about teamwork?

What have you learned yourself about how to make teamwork work better next time?

Applying what you have learned

Skills focus
✓ Reflection

Learning focus
• Reflect on learning, communication and collaborating (working in a group).

Your task

You will work in a group to tell a story about values and human rights by using two techniques from drama: freeze frame and action clips.

Approaching the task

Your group can practise telling the story by improvising a few freeze frames and action clips together.

• A freeze frame is when your group creates a single scene that expresses a single important moment from your story, frozen in time. You can choose to have a narrator who 'sets the scene' by explaining in one or two sentences what the story is about.

• An action clip unfreezes the action. Characters from the freeze frame can move and speak. The action freezes again once your teacher (or the narrator) shouts 'Freeze!'

To decide on your story:

• Look back at your group's top five articles from the UDHR (Unit 5.1). This will help you pick a human right to focus on.

• Look back at your group's list of shared values (Unit 5.1) and your group's logo (if you designed one). This will help you decide what value or values your story will illustrate.

• Eleanor Roosevelt said about human rights beginning in small places, close to home. What might this mean for your story?

Really think about what your poses in the freeze frame are expressing.

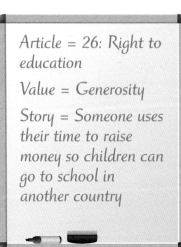

Article = 24: Right to rest and leisure

Value = Justice

Story = Someone makes sure their work colleagues get a break

Article = 26: Right to education

Value = Generosity

Story = Someone uses their time to raise money so children can go to school in another country

Article = 29: Community duties and responsibilities

Value = Courage

Story = Someone stands up for others when they are facing discrimination

Plan and practise:

- Plan your freeze frame. It should show a critical point in your story. Everyone in your group needs a role (of course!).

- Each character in the freeze frame should think about their backstory – who are they? What is important to them? What would they say about the story?

- Prepare for the action clip as well as the freeze frame. When you unfreeze, what will each character do to continue the story: think about both movement as well as what they will say.

- Practise your freeze frame and what happens when you unfreeze.

Perform.

- Each group should perform their freeze frame and action clip to the rest of the class.

- The other groups should give feedback after each performance.

Reflecting on your progress

This is another group activity, so it is an opportunity for your group to improve the way you work together as a team:

- Reflect on the feedback your group received from the rest of the class for your team-building activity.

- Reflect on what your group decided it would try to improve from the lessons learned meeting.

- You could also check your progress on reflection now – see the next page for objectives.

We started this unit with a thought from Aristotle. He expressed his idea this way:

> It is well said, then, that it is by doing **just acts** that the just man is produced… without doing these no one would have even a **prospect** of becoming good.

What might you do in your daily life to **uphold** the values that are most important to you?

Study skills

Look back at the sentence starters in Unit 5.4 for ideas to get started with reflection.

What is your teacher looking for?

Your group should be able to explain what you are looking to improve in your group work this time, and how you are carrying this out.

Vocabulary

just acts: acting in a way that is considered morally correct and fair

prospect: possibility or likelihood

uphold: support something by doing it

Check your progress

Beginning	Developing	Going beyond
• I can listen to others in class discussions and share my own ideas and questions.	• I can listen to ideas and information about an issue and ask questions about it.	• I can listen to ideas and information and ask questions and make points that show how much I understand.
• I can work well with my team, suggesting ideas that help us complete our team task together.	• I can work well with my team, suggesting useful ideas and solving problems to help us complete our team task together.	• I can work well with my team, suggesting useful ideas, solving problems and encouraging other team members in a way that helps us complete our team task together.
• I can present information about an issue clearly, using good organisation.	• I can present information about an issue clearly, using good organisation and with some references for my sources.	• I can present information about an issue clearly and with reasons, using good organisation and with some references for my sources.
• I can say how working together has improved how we did our task.	• I can say what was good about the way we worked together, and what the challenges were.	• I can weigh up what was good about the way we worked together, and what the challenges were.

Next steps

- There are lots and lots of books, blogs, websites, podcasts and videos about improving teamwork. Why not write or record your own guide to successful teamwork?
- Work as a team to plan a class, year or whole-school event to celebrate Human Rights Day (10 December).

Finding solutions
Working in teams, being a leader and getting the job done

6

If you were making something that had lots of stages to the process, would it be better if you did all those stages yourself? Or would it work better if you just focused on one stage and worked as part of a team of people, with each person completing a particular stage? For that team to be effective, would it need a manager?

In this chapter, you will be exploring the topic of 'Employment'. The issues you will be considering include:

- **What's in a job?**
- **What makes a team more effective?**
- **Could you be the boss? What is involved in leading a team?**
- **How is the world of work changing?**

You will be developing a range of collaboration, analysis and reflection skills:

6.1 Collaborating in a team

6.2 Improving teamwork

6.3 Reflecting on the skills to make a team work well

6.4 Analysing the world of work

6.5 Applying what you have learned.

Your final task will be to plan how a team could successfully tackle a project, build the skills of its members, and achieve an outcome.

Collaborating in a team

Skills focus
✓ Collaboration
Learning focus
- Assign roles and divide tasks fairly to achieve a shared outcome.
- Contribute useful ideas to support teamwork.
- Encourage team members to participate and resolve any issues.

Big question: What's in a job?

Getting started

All of us do something during our lives that counts as work – and some of us do a lot of it! It may be that you've already had a job – or that you have one now. Your work might be paid, or it might be something you do to help around the home or support a family member.

1. Are you a 'team player' – do you find it easier or more enjoyable to work as part of a group, or are you better working on your own, so you can do things the way you think best?

Exploring

Minaj is a bus driver in Nepal; he works on the same route every day. Let's see what he thinks about his job.

The best thing about my job: It's a steady income and I like the people I meet.

The worst thing about it: When the traffic is bad. Also, some roads are in a poor condition, so the bus breaks down – then everyone thinks I'm a bad driver!

The people I work with: The other drivers are great – we always help each other out. The passengers are friendly, too!

Could anyone do my job?: No, not really! The buses are big and heavy, so it takes skill to drive them well – that comes with practice. You need to be patient, too.

Do I want to keep my job?: I suppose I could become a manager – that would mean more money, but more work! I like being out on the road, so I'll stay with this for now – but more money would be nice.

2 Think about a job that you know something about.

a) Working on your own, go through the questions Minaj was asked and think about how you would answer them.

b) Then join with a partner and compare your ideas.

c) Together, make notes in response to these questions:

- What qualities make a job great?

- Do lots of jobs have the same bad points?

- Should a person always do the same job?

- How do the skills people have influence their choice of job?

Most people collaborate with others in the work they do. Sometimes they may work as part of a team, but even if people work alone, they may have to interact with others in different ways.

You have been given the job of planting seedlings, working in a group of four. The instructions for planting are:

1. Dig small hole.
2. Insert seedling into hole.
3. Pack soil around seedling.
4. Water seedling.

You can organise the work however you like. Two ideas for how to do this are shown in Plan A and Plan B below.

Plan A

- Divide the seedlings into four groups.

- Each person works with their own set of seedlings to follow the instructions.

Plan B

Divide the tasks across four people:

- One person digs the holes.

- The second person puts in the seedlings.

- The third person packs down the soil.

- The fourth person waters the seedlings.

3 Working in a group, discuss the best way of planting the seedlings. Give reasons for your answers.

a) Which would be the quickest way of working – Plan A or Plan B?

b) Which would result in the plants being planted most effectively?

c) Which approach would you prefer to use?

Developing

Here are two people talking about Plans A and B:

> I prefer Plan A. I get the satisfaction of planting my seedlings. I look at them and think 'I did that!'

> I prefer Plan B. You can work quicker if you're just doing one part. You get good at it, and you get really quick as well.

4 Working on your own, make notes in response to these questions.

a) Is personal satisfaction important when you're doing a job?

b) Why might working quickly be important?

c) How good do you think you are at working under pressure?

d) What are the advantages and disadvantages of working in a team?

5 You are going to work individually to make a small toy. You will be provided with a sheet that needs to be coloured in, cut out, folded and assembled.

When you have finished, reflect on your experience.

a) Did you do a good job?

b) What was difficult?

c) Did each stage take the same amount of time?

Toys need to be made to a certain standard or customers will reject them.

6 Working in a group, make notes in response to these questions.

a) What are the features of a well-assembled toy?

b) Is it better for people to check the toys they've made themselves, or for other people to check them?

c) What skills do you need to be good at checking toy quality?

d) Could you make toys to a higher standard if you did all the stages yourself, or if you worked as a team with each person carrying out just one function?

Final task

7 You are going to make the small toy again, but this time you will organise yourselves as a team with specific roles. So, you need a plan of action!

a) Work in a group to consider your responses to the following questions:

- How could you solve the problem of some stages taking longer than others?

- Who in the team has particular skills that would be helpful for each particular stage?

b) Draw up your team plan. It should clearly indicate who does what and the order that jobs will be done in.

- Consider the skills that people need to perform each role effectively.

- Make sure that every team member is clear about their role.

c) When your plan is complete, show it to other teams and compare it with theirs.

- Have they thought of things that your group hasn't thought of?

- Have you had some ideas they want to use?

d) Rework your plan based on any new ideas and feedback, then set it out neatly.

❓ REFLECTION POINT

Read these two ideas about working in teams.

> I've seen our plan and it's great. I only have one job to do, so I can just do that. I don't need to know what anyone else is doing or whether they are doing it well.

> I don't think we need a plan. Working as a group is great, but we can all just do a bit of everything. Whatever needs doing next – we can just pick it up and do it.

What do you think of these ideas about working in teams? What would you say to each of these people?

Improving teamwork

Skills focus
✓ Collaboration
✓ Reflection
Learning focus
- Work positively within a team to achieve a shared outcome.
- Improve teamwork, for example by contributing useful ideas, encouraging participation and resolving conflict.

Big question: What makes a team more effective?

Getting started

In the previous unit, you worked together as a team to plan how you would make as many high-quality toys as possible within a specified time.

1 Each team is now going into production.

a) You will be assembling high-quality toys that the customer will be happy with, and you need to do so as quickly as possible.

b) Use the plan you prepared in Unit 6.1 to guide your organisation.

c) You are in competition with the other teams in the room: you will all have the same amount of time, but remember – you are aiming for quality as well as quantity.

Exploring

After completing a group task, effective teams spend time considering how well they performed and whether they could do better next time.

2 So, how well did your team do? Working on your own, note down your responses to these questions.

a) How many high-quality toys did your team assemble?

b) How did your team's **output** compare with the output of the other teams?

c) Who in the team was well employed, and who was underemployed?

d) Were there any **bottlenecks** – and how well did you sort them out?

e) How valued did each team member feel?

f) If you were repeating the task again, would you use the same plan?

> ### Vocabulary
>
> **output**: the amount of something produced – in this case, the number of toys
>
> **bottleneck**: any situation that causes a delay at one point in a process or system

A useful way of thinking about how well you worked together as a team is to use a PMI grid. This stands for 'Plus, Minus, Interesting'.

3 **a)** Read the example PMI grid below. Look carefully at both the headings and the examples.

Plus (list any positive features)	Minus (list any negative features)	Interesting (list any interesting points to consider for next time)
We had two people cutting out who were quick and accurate.	If the slots were too small, it was tricky to get the tabs in – this slowed us down.	People might feel more motivated and less bored if they sometimes change job.

b) As a group, complete a PMI grid for your team's work during the toy assembly task. Aim to include at least three points in each column.

Some people adapt to teamworking quite easily, whereas others prefer to work alone. But being a team member shouldn't be a **passive** role – it's important to contribute.

In addition to getting the job done well, people often want to feel fulfilled in their job and valued by the people they work with.

> **Vocabulary**
>
> **passive**: allowing other people to do things for you; the opposite of being active

4 Working on your own, note down your responses to these questions.

a) Think about your role in the team – did you feel successful?

b) Was your role fulfilling?

c) Did you feel valued by other team members?

d) Share your views with the rest of the team and discuss your responses.

5 Now reflect on your discussion within the team.

a) How easy was it to give other people feedback on what went well?

b) How easy was it to discuss problems the team had?

c) What communication skills worked well when giving feedback?

Developing

'Kaizen' is a Japanese process, developed in manufacturing industries, especially electronics (Sony) and cars (Toyota). Kaizen involves making small improvements to the quality of a product.

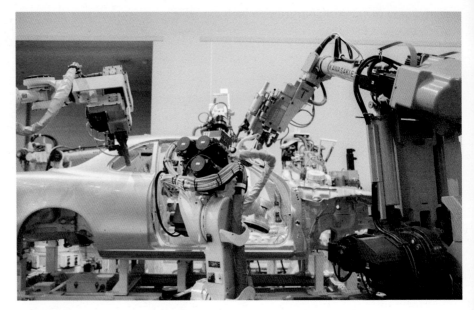

- Changes are often suggested by the workforce.

- They rarely involve major change or significant investment.

- They are therefore easy to implement.

Workers are encouraged to take ownership of these changes, so they feel involved and valued.

6 Look at the example of how the kaizen process could be applied to the toy assembly activity. Then discuss these questions with a partner:

a) How well do you think the problem identified in the chart was solved?

b) How useful is a chart like this for analysing problems and devising solutions?

<1> Problem to be solved	Slots sometimes not cut properly, so tabs didn't fit. This stopped the assembly line until slots had been enlarged.
<2> Actions to be taken	1. Use scissors with sharper points so easier to cut full-size slots. 2. Train people so they know how to cut slots.
<3> People involved	Adam and Zack (on cutting-out duties)
<4> Resources needed	1. Sharper pointed scissors 2. Time to carry out training
<5> Intended outcome/result	Well-cut slots that tabs fit into straightaway
<6> Monitoring – did this change work?	Fairly well. New scissors were effective. Adam improved, but Zack struggles with scissor control so had to swap roles.

Sometimes changes need to be made in the way a team works to make it more effective. Managing these changes well is essential to the success of the team.

7 Discuss these questions in a group.

a) How might Adam be feeling about the changes?

b) How might Zack be feeling?

c) What strategies could help Zack feel positive about his role in the team?

Final task

8 a) Working on your own, apply the kaizen process to your team's experience of the toy assembly activity.

- Identify a problem your team experienced with assembling the toys.

- Complete a chart like the one on page 106, to show how you might solve the problem.

- Suggest why one (or more) team members might not like the changes you are proposing.

- Offer a way of dealing with this so that the whole team remains positive.

b) Now join up with the other members of your team and compare your completed charts. Decide between yourselves which actions will bring about a greater improvement.

c) Develop a group chart that identifies and proposes solutions to three different problems.

d) Share your group's chart with the rest of the class. You could put the charts on display and look at each other's work. Do other groups have solutions that you think you might be able to use?

❓ REFLECTION POINT

Spend a few minutes on your own thinking about the teamwork you have done in this unit.

- How well did you collaborate as a team in the final task?

- Which aspects of teamwork do your team need to improve on – for example, working under pressure, undertaking repetitive tasks, maintaining attention to detail?

- Which aspects of teamwork did you find particularly challenging?

- Think about how team members responded to feedback within the team. What went well and what did people find difficult? How could this process be improved upon?

Reflecting on the skills to make a team work well

Skills focus
✓ Reflection
Learning focus
- Explain personal contribution to teamwork.
- Reflect on ways of managing teams more effectively.
- Identify targets for improvement.

Big question: Could you be the boss? What is involved in leading a team?

Getting started

1 Think about your experiences of having or being a manager. Working with a partner, discuss:

a) What do you think are the qualities of a good manager?

b) If someone was managing you, how should they do it?

Exploring

Imagine your team is going to do the toy assembly activity again but this time with you as the manager. As team manager, you won't be doing any of the assembly work. Instead, you will be observing the process, identifying and sorting problems, allocating roles, organising people and watching how well they perform. You will need to keep everyone focused and motivated. At the end of the task, you will be judged on the team's performance.

2 How well do you think you would do?

Copy and then complete this questionnaire to show your responses. You will need to seek feedback from the other members of your team for questions b and d.

3 Based on your responses, what skills do you need to develop to be a good manager? Aim to come up with an action plan with at least five points. For example:

A Ways in which I would make a good manager:	B Ways in which other people think I would make a good manager:
C Things I would need to work on to be a good manager:	D Things other people think I would need to work on to be a good manager:

Think of ways to motivate people to do a task they find boring.

Some people think that if you are doing something in a team and the team is working well, then three things should be happening – see the diagram.

☐ You achieved the task. For example, a good team would have assembled lots of toy cars that were made well.

☐ Your team is stronger as a result of doing the task. For example, you supported each other as a team.

☐ You developed as an individual. For example, you learned something new or improved a key skill.

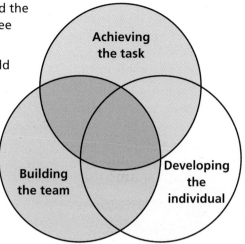

The three elements needed to ensure a team is working well.

4 Working in your group, discuss your responses to these questions.

a) How well do you think your team achieved the task?

b) Did your team feel stronger for doing the activity?

c) Did the toy assembly task enable you to develop individually?

d) If you had had a manager for the toy assembly activity, would these three outcomes have been better? Sketch a copy of the diagram and annotate it to show your thinking.

Developing

5 Read through the job advert below and discuss your responses with a partner.

a) What skills does this team leader need? Make a list.

b) How many of these skills do you have?

c) For any skills that you don't have, how could you solve this problem?

Team leader required for mountain challenge!

Team manager required to lead a team across a challenging mountain landscape to refit a shelter used by climbers. The hut can only be accessed on foot after several hours' hiking across boggy areas and through streams.

The structure of the hut is good, but it needs cleaning, and broken furniture and equipment require repair.

You will need to carry any tools to make repairs along with any supplies for the trip.

6   As well as you as the team leader, the mountain team will
consist of three other people. You have five **applicants** and
must select the three you will take. The details of the five
applicants are below.

a) Study the details carefully. Thinking about these broader
skills, which ones do you think would be particularly
valuable for the mountain hut repair team?

b) Decide which three people you will select for the team.
Working on your own, make a note of the three people you
have chosen.

	Job role	Skills	Less experienced at	General fitness level
Applicant 1	Carpenter	Working with wood and other materials	Working as part of a team	Good – strong
Applicant 2	Fitness coach	Managing fitness levels of teams and motivating people	Project planning	Excellent, though less used to challenging landscapes
Applicant 3	Mountain leader	Leading groups to travel across challenging terrains	Craft skills and shaping materials	Good, especially in terms of stamina
Applicant 4	Interior designer	Using variety of materials to fit buildings out for range of purposes	Working in challenging environments	Very good – used to working out in the gym
Applicant 5	Builder	Construction and repair work both internal and external	Responding to unexpected problems	Very good – keen swimmer

c) Now share your ideas within your group. Explain why you want the people that you have selected and see what other people think. Come to a group decision.

d) Your group should now compare its recommendations with those of other groups.

- Is there any candidate you all agree on?

- Can you agree as a class on the ideal team?

Many people work in teams in the jobs they do. When you are selected for a job, it's likely that whoever selected you decided that you would work well with the rest of the team.

When you were selecting the mountain hut repair team, you not only had to consider each individual but also how they would complement each other as a group. Of course, you had to select people on very limited information – in practice, you would probably know more about them.

7 a) Think of three other questions you could ask the applicants to gather useful information that would help you decide.

b) Share your questions as a group. Did other people have questions that would be helpful in making a final decision?

Final task

Managing a team is an important skill and there are many parts to it. They include being able to make good decisions and to recognise skills that different people have.

8 Working on your own:

a) Summarise the skills you think are needed to be a manager. Write a list.

b) Think about what you have learned about managing teams. Note down three key points you think are important.

c) Look back at Units 6.1 and 6.2 where you were learning about effective collaboration, team working and communication skills. As a manager, how could you motivate people to do these things well? Note down three ways of doing this.

❓ REFLECTION POINT

Consider the list of management skills you made.

- Which of those are your strengths and which are your development areas? Highlight them in different colours.

- For each development area, suggest something you could do or learn about to help you improve.

Analysing the world of work

Big question: How is the world of work changing?

Getting started

1 Note down your responses to these questions.

 a) What do you think has changed about work over the last 10 years or more?

 b) What has stayed the same?

 c) Are jobs now better – or worse – than 10 years ago? Explain your thinking.

Exploring

The nature of employment is constantly adapting to a changing world. This affects people in all types of jobs.

2 Read the article on the opposite page on how the world of work is changing today – and how it is set to change in the future.

 These ideas came from an article written by Alain Dehaze, **CEO** of the Adecco Group, a large multinational corporation that provides other organisations with both temporary and permanent staff.

3 Working with a partner, discuss the reliability of this article.

 a) Is the Adecco Group likely to know about trends in the workplace?

 b) Why might you conclude that the opinions in this article are valid?

 c) Why might you have some reservations about the validity of the article?

Predicting what might happen in the future is difficult, but it can be useful to try. Predictions tend to be driven by two main factors:

- identifying recent trends and assuming they will continue; for example, there is a trend in many countries for people to move from rural to urban areas

- identifying events that may change or upset trends; for example, several countries have announced future bans on the sale of new petrol and diesel cars.

Vocabulary

CEO: Chief Executive Officer; the person responsible for running a large business

ethnicity: a person's sense of belonging to a particular cultural or national group

inclusive: providing opportunity for all people to be included

Key trends in the workplace for the coming year

1. A lack of talent

Training is an issue. Employers often need workers with key skills but are struggling to recruit people with the required skill sets.

2. Switch to greener working

The climate crisis is changing our world and employment patterns. Efforts are also being made to reduce our reliance on fossil fuels, for example through solar panel technology and a switch to electric vehicles.

3. Digital transformation

Digital technology has already changed many areas of work, including the ability to work from home and self-scan machines replacing staff. This trend is set to continue.

4. Retaining valuable workers

Sometimes people want to move and change jobs. This brings new ideas and experiences into a workplace, but it can disrupt work and makes the organisation less effective.

5. Equity, equality and inclusion

Many people think gender and **ethnicity** shouldn't influence a person's work opportunities. However, in many industries women earn less than men, and some ethnic groups are under-represented and under-rewarded.

6. Leaders being transparent and accountable

There is increasing pressure on business leaders to be clear about where they stand in relation to key issues in the world, such as climate change and **inclusive** working practices.

Source: Adapted from '6 world of work trends set to shape 2022', World Economic Forum in collaboration with The Adecco Group, 2022.

---

4 Working in a group, note down your responses to these ideas:

a) What training and qualifications might you need to realise your future hopes and plans?

b) If a good job came up in a different location, would you move?

c) How might industries near you change in relation to greener working?

d) What role might digital technology play in your future job?

5 If you had a job, would you expect your boss to be honest about:

a) the decisions they had made?

b) matters such as pay and future prospects?

6 Imagine you are the boss of a large organisation. You read the article about key trends in the workplace for the coming year.

a) Consider the impact on your workforce of:

- the information about talent and training

- the current trends towards digitisation and home working.

b) How could you make your organisation one that workers want to be part of?

Developing

7 A multinational corporation is proposing to build a new factory in a less industrialised country. Read through local people's reactions to the proposed new factory.

> The factory will bring lots of jobs to the area.

> Local shops and businesses will benefit as the people working in the factory will have more money to spend.

> The company doesn't care about local people – it will end up exploiting them.

> The company is only coming to our country because local people are cheap to employ.

> Local people will learn a lot of new skills.

> Setting up the factory will benefit the area in other ways – roads will be improved and there will be more local services.

> The factory will make lots of money – but none of it will stay in our country.

8 Will the factory benefit the local community? Working on your own, copy and complete the table below to help you decide.

Strong arguments in support of the factory:	Strong arguments to oppose the factory:
Weaker arguments in support of the factory:	**Weaker arguments to oppose the factory:**

The government of the country agrees to the new factory. It will provide well-paid jobs for local workers, and they will learn new skills.

However, although the workers are local, most of the managers have come from abroad. The company says the locals don't have the management skills. The managers get paid a lot more and some don't speak the local language.

Some of the workers feel they are being underpaid. They are threatening to go on strike. The company says that if they do, the factory will close.

9 Working with a partner, discuss:

a) What problems can you see arising?

b) What do you think the workers should do?

Final task

10 The factory has been operating for several years. You have now been asked to make recommendations to the owners about how to make sure the factory continues to be successful. They have read the article about future workforce trends (page 113) and want to know how to respond.

Working in a group, look at the six areas identified in the article and prepare a report. Your report should make recommendations to the factory owners in each area, indicating what they should be doing to help the factory develop for the future.

- Decide how to divide up the different aspects of the task between your group.

- You may wish to do some further research on some of the six areas in the article.

- Remember to use clear **evidence** to support your **arguments**.

❓ REFLECTION POINT

Think back over the work you have done in this unit.

a) Suggest three things that will be different about the workplace 25 years from now.

b) Suggest three things that will not change.

For each point you make, briefly explain your ideas.

🔑 Key terms

evidence: information about a global issue that helps to develop understanding or prove that something is true or false

argument: a series of statements containing reasons and evidence which support a claim about a global issue

Applying what you have learned

Your task

You will work in a group to plan a business that makes and sells greetings cards.

Approaching the task

You decide to set up a business that makes and sells greetings cards. You realise that in many countries, when people send cards, they like them to be a bit different. The idea is that the cards will be unique and draw upon the talents of local artists.

The cards need to be designed, printed, folded and provided with an envelope. A local printing firm will print the cards; all the other aspects of producing the cards will be done within your own team.

You can't afford a large workforce to begin with – you can only afford to employ 10 workers, so you will need to think carefully about the jobs they will do.

1. Spend some time thinking about the various roles you will need on your team. You'll need to think about the work that needs doing – and it may be that you'll need several people in one role.

    a) Working on your own, decide how to allocate the 10 roles for the card-making business. Sketch out a plan for the workforce.

    b) Share your plan with others in the group. Discuss your ideas and come up with a group plan. Present your group plan as a poster, so that other people in the class can see what you've thought of.

    c) Look at the posters other groups have made. Did they have similar ideas to you – or have they had different ideas you could use? Return to your group and discuss whether you want to update your plan in any way.

2 To be successful, the card business is going to need a manager.

    a) Working in your group, record your responses to these questions:

- What skills and experience should you be looking for when recruiting someone to manage the business?

- Should the manager have the skills to do any of the other jobs in the team, or do they just need to be good at managing people?

    b) Based on the results of your discussion, create a **job profile** for the manager of the card business.

Vocabulary

job profile: a description of the tasks involved in doing a specific job

3 The flow chart below gives some ideas for the different stages in the design and production of the cards. The flow chart is not as good as it could be – for example, it doesn't have anything in it about advertising or promoting the cards.

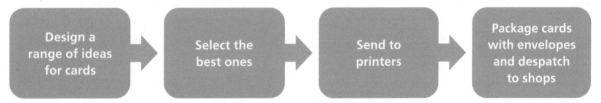

In your team, draw up a better flow diagram for the design and production of the cards. Make sure every job role you identified for the card-making business is included.

4 **a)** How might the card-making business develop in the future?

    Look back at the article in Unit 6.4 about how the world of work is changing. Identify any factors that might influence the business and bring about changes.

    b) Make five predictions for how the card-making business will change in the next 10 years.

Reflecting on your progress

1 Consider your contribution in this group activity.

    a) What role did you play in the team?

    b) Were your ideas used?

    c) How did you encourage and support others?

    d) How did you deal with differences in points of view?

    e) What could the team have done better?

2 How have your teamworking and collaboration skills improved since the toy assembly activity in Unit 6.1?

Check your progress

Beginning	Developing	Going beyond
• I experienced working in a team and can talk about what worked well and what could have been improved.	• I worked in a team and analysed how well it succeeded, offering ideas and suggestions about possible improvements.	• I analysed my experience of working in a team and fulfilled a number of the roles within that team.
• I can discuss my ideas about what a good team leader is like and the skills you might look for in other team members.	• I analysed a range of job roles within a team, including team leader, and suggested the skills necessary to complete a task.	• I suggested a comprehensive set of skills needed to succeed in a task and matched these to available workers.
• I know some of the ways in which the world of work is changing.	• I applied some ideas about the changing world of work to my own knowledge and experience.	• I recognised changes in working practices in my local area and used these to support a wider analysis of changes in the world of work.

Next steps

- Think about your own profile of employment skills, including those you feel are your strengths and those you want to develop. Look for opportunities to expand and improve your skill set.

- Seek opportunities to talk to or observe people who work in teams. Find out what they need to do to succeed in those situations. Consider the individual skills they bring and also how they build on the skills of other people to strengthen the group.

- Find out about local employment opportunities in your area and see who is recruiting. Do they seem to be small local businesses, medium-sized organisations or large international companies? See if you can find out what kind of jobs they offer and what skills they are looking for. What seems to be in demand?

Bringing your skills together

How should we conserve our natural environment?

Conservation – protecting the environment from the damaging effects of human activities – is a global concern. Who can tell us how to fix this problem? Consider the main features of your local park or walk – such as a river or woodland. How do we protect these areas from damage? What projects can we do to help?

In this chapter, you will be exploring the topic of 'Environment, pollution and conservation'. The issues you will be considering include:

- **Who is interested in the state of our local environment?**

- **Why does our natural environment need maintenance?**

- **How can we research putting a plan together?**

- **What can young people do to help?**

You will be revising and practising the evaluation, analysis, research, communication and reflection skills that you have learned:

7.1 Evaluating different sources

7.2 Evaluating and applying an argument

7.3 Applying what you have learned: conducting primary research

7.4 Applying what you have learned: presenting your goal

7.5 Reflecting on what you have learned.

Your final task will be to write a personal reflection on what you have learned about the topic of conservation, presenting arguments and group collaboration.

Evaluating different sources

Skills focus
✓ Evaluation
Learning focus
• Evaluate different sources analysing the same issue.
• Recognise bias and explore credibility.

Big question: What's wrong with our lake?

Getting started

Are rivers and lakes an important feature of your local environment?

1 Working in a group, identify an important natural feature where you live (for example, a forest, beach or mountain).

a) What is the natural feature like?

b) Who uses it for leisure activities?

c) Why is the natural environment important for your local area?

d) Is there anything that prevents your locality from being as 'natural' as it could be?

Exploring

2 Read this article about a problem in a park in St Albans, a city in the UK. The article appeared in a local newspaper.

Floods and mud: what's happening with Verulamium Lake?
by Laura Bill

What's happening with Verulamium Lake? That's the question being asked by a local politician unhappy with the state of the district landmark.

The **opposition councillor** believes the jewel in St Albans' crown is being neglected and said residents have been raising their concerns with him.

Councillor Aaron Jacob at Verulamium Lake.

'There seem to be **persistent** issues with the lake in Verulamium Park. On a walk this morning, I saw that one area has been sectioned off due to slippery paths.

'On walks to the park during the second and third lockdowns [in the Covid-19 pandemic in 2020–21], the flooding of the lake prevented everyone from using the paths and they clearly were not accessible to everyone. The council doesn't seem to be able to **get on top of** the flooding afflicting the park.

'Verulamium Park is an amazing community **asset** which we should all treasure. I want to see more action here to ensure that the pathways remain open and accessible to everyone in our community.'

[…] The council's head of community services said: 'The recent flooding at Verulamium Park was due to exceptionally high rainfall and was outside of our control.

'The **Environment Agency**, which has responsibility for managing flood risk on the River Ver, has classified part of the park as a **flood plain** and so unfortunately this sort of flooding can be expected from time to time.

'Only a small section of the footpaths, around 30 metres long by the boating lake, remains closed because it is still flooded and there is also some **subsidence**. We are continuing to monitor this section.'

A multi-million pound project known as Revitalising the River Ver is being spearheaded by the Environment Agency […]. Proposals include reshaping the main lake and reducing it by a third in order to make room for a new stream flowing through the park.

Source: *The Herts Advertiser*, 2 September 2021.

3 Working on your own or with a partner, answer these questions to evaluate the reliability of the account given in the article.

a) How does the article call readers' attention to the problem?

b) Does the article begin with facts or an opinion?

c) Why might an opposition politician not be a reliable source?

d) Can you find examples of **assertion** and **bias** in the article?

e) To what extent is a council spokesperson a reliable source?

f) What are the facts in the article?

g) What are the proposed solutions to the problem with the lake?

Vocabulary

opposition councillor: elected local representative for a political party that is opposed to those in charge

persistent: recurring or repeating

get on top of: sort out or deal with

asset: something of value

Environment Agency: UK government action group set up to protect the environment

flood plain: area near a river that is expected to flood at times of high water

subsidence: when ground sinks

Key terms

assertion: a confident statement of fact or belief

bias: favouring one person or point of view over another in a way considered to be unfair

Study skills

For a reminder about evaluating sources and bias, see Unit 2.4.

4 Read this article, which was published later on the local government website.

a) Why might this article be *more* reliable than an independent local newspaper?

b) In what ways might it be *less* reliable than an independent local newspaper?

Revitalising the River Ver

The River Ver, St Albans.

The River Ver flows through Verulamium Park and the heart of the city of St Albans. It is one of around only 200 chalk rivers in the entire world.

Chalk rivers are fed from the chalk **aquifer** (the underground layer of rock saturated with groundwater). They are naturally crystal clear and support a huge diversity of habitats and wildlife. Their rarity and importance have led them to be described as 'England's Rainforest'.

Unfortunately, like many chalk rivers, the River Ver has fallen into a bad state. In St Albans, the river channel has been heavily modified over the years. This has led to an artificially over-wide, over-straight channel and **sluggish** flows. These alterations contribute to the **gravel** bed being smothered with a thick layer of **silt**.

The river is also unable to support the **iconic** chalk stream plants we would like to see. One reason is that the channel is also overshadowed by trees which prevents light reaching the river and allowing chalk river plants to thrive.

Verulamium Park Lakes

Built in the 1930s, the iconic ornamental lakes of Verulamium Park are also in a bad way. They are far too large for the flow they receive and are clogged with silt. The large numbers of non-native Canada geese add to this issue as their droppings contribute to the poor water quality.

Mission statement

To deliver a publicly supported, award-winning project and **legacy** on time and within budget through collaboration and efficient communication.

Vocabulary

Revitalising: restoring to its original natural state

aquifer: underground rock layers that contain water

sluggish: slow moving

gravel: collection of small stones

silt: mud at the bottom of water that does not flow

iconic: valued and important

legacy: something to be passed on to the next generation

Source: St Albans City and District Council.

5 Working on your own, make notes in response to the following questions.

   a) Does this article begin with an opinion or a fact?

   b) Why does it begin with the river and not the lake?

   c) Why are chalk rivers an important environmental asset?

   d) Which is more important, the state of the lake or the state of the river?

   e) Which Global Perspectives skills will the council need to carry out its conservation project to clean up the River Ver successfully?

Different sources are not necessarily better or more reliable, but they have different audiences and purposes.

6 Work with a partner to evaluate how the information on the webpage compares with the newspaper article. For each source, consider:

   • its purpose

   • its intended audience

   • how this affects the way the content is presented

   • whether facts are presented accurately (source reliability)

   • whether opinions are based on **evidence** (source credibility)

   • the balance between fact and opinion.

Final task

7 Work with a partner to consider the **arguments** for and against the project to change the course of the river and shrink the size of the lakes. One of you can explore all the arguments in favour and one of you all the arguments against. Which of you has the better arguments?

Once you have agreed, draft a joint letter to the newspaper replying to their article after reading the website. Express your opinion about whether a conservation project for the river and shrinking the size of the lakes would be a good or a bad idea.

> **Key terms**
>
> **evidence**: information about a global issue that helps to develop understanding or prove that something is true or false
>
> **argument**: a series of statements containing reasons and evidence which support a claim about a global issue

? REFLECTION POINT

How could you learn about conservation issues in your local community? Where could you research sources of information about them?

Evaluating and applying an argument

Learning focus
- Discuss the effectiveness of an argument's structure and use of evidence.
- Make connections between global and local problems.
- Explain causes and consequences to others.

Big question: How can local action make a global difference?

Getting started

Global Perspectives involves thinking globally but acting locally. You have looked at a local problem in the city of St Albans in the UK, but how does it reflect global issues and concerns?

1. Read the article about freshwater **ecosystems**. Then with a partner, discuss these questions and list your responses.

   a) Why is water so important?

   b) How has the way we use water changed in recent times?

   c) What are the consequences of human activity for freshwater species?

   d) What are the issues with conservation and biodiversity in your local community?

> ### Vocabulary
>
> **ecosystem**: all the living and non-living things in an area such as plants, animals, water, soil
>
> **wetland**: land made up of marshes or swamps
>
> **degrade**: lower the quality of
>
> **biodiversity**: the variety of plant and animal species living in an area
>
> **headwater**: stream or streams that are the source of a river

---

The planet's freshwater ecosystems are in crisis: research found that populations of monitored freshwater species have fallen by 84 per cent and nearly one-third of **wetland** ecosystems have been lost since 1970 due to human activities that **degrade** habitats and decrease water quality.

But despite their vital contributions to humans and **biodiversity**, freshwater ecosystems receive only a small percentage of the funding dedicated to nature conservation, explained Robin Abell, a co-author of a recent review of these findings published in the journal Science, who leads Conservation International's freshwater work.

'Freshwater ecosystems connect **headwaters** with oceans, land with water and people with the resources they need to thrive,' Abell said. 'However, they have historically been ignored during the development of conservation initiatives such as protected areas and other management interventions.'

Source: Conservation International.

Exploring

2 Read this article about the River Ver from a local conservation group website. As you read, consider how the text connects this local issue with global concerns.

ABOUT THE AUTHORS   ARCHIVE   **NEWS**   VIDEOS   CONTACT ▾

The River Ver and Its People

Humankind has always relied on clean, fresh water for ourselves and our animals, in the past taking it straight from the river. However, steadily increasing demands on water resources over the second half of the last century meant that supplies had to be drawn from deep in the chalk aquifer by means of **boreholes**. This is ground water which would normally feed into the river.

Now at the start of the 21st century further large areas of the country have been designated for new house building. Statistics show continued increase in water consumption **per head**. However, the Ver Valley Society is striving to increase awareness of the **impending ecological** problems that this demand for water will cause, especially at a time when climate change poses its own threat.

The Ver must not be allowed to **dwindle away** as it nearly did in the early 1990s.

Apart from the air we breathe, water is probably the most important thing in life. None of us could live very long without it. We can live longer without food than we can without water. In the Ver catchment for example, each of us uses over 150 litres per day for washing, drinking and cleaning – despite a compulsory water meter programme being introduced recently.

Did you know?

Fresh water is one of the Earth's most precious resources.

Water covers over 70 per cent of our planet's surface but only 3 per cent of this is fresh water and two-thirds of that is held in the polar ice caps. Therefore, only 1 per cent of the total is available for rivers, lakes, wetlands and human consumption.

Vocabulary

borehole: deep hole drilled into the ground when searching for water

per head: per person

impending: will happen soon

ecological: relating to living things and the environments in which they live

dwindle away: become less; decrease in size

Source: Ver Valley Society.

3 Working with a partner, evaluate and make notes on how the article about the River Ver moves from a local problem to discussing a global issue.

   a) Does the article begin with a local or a global statement?

   b) What national changes have put pressure on the local resource?

   c) How does the article link this pressure to other global problems?

   d) How are the problems of the river linked to problems in the supply of fresh water?

   e) Where is there evidence of research in the article?

   f) Where are facts and information presented?

   g) Does the article end with a global point or a local point?

   h) How does it encourage you, as reader, to think about your own behaviour?

4 Now decide together how well structured this website article is.

   a) Will it attract the audience it wants?

   b) Does it convince you that local problems are related to global issues?

   c) What does it encourage the reader to do or think about?

   Feed back your opinions to the rest of the class.

Developing

5 Working in a group, use your notes to evaluate how the article supports its argument. What evidence does it use to explain causes and consequences? Consider:

   a) Why are facts important in developing a persuasive argument for change?

   b) How did the article persuade you that chalk rivers are important?

   c) Why is this a conservation issue?

   d) How far did the first article about freshwater ecosystems and the second article about the River Ver convince you that humans need to change our attitudes to water?

   e) Decide in your group what the second article persuades you to do. What is its purpose, and does it succeed?

   f) Present your evaluation of the article to the rest of the class. (You will need to decide as a group on the role each member will have in the presentation.)

> **Study skills**
>
> You may wish to revisit what you learned about roles within a group in Unit 4.5.

Final task

6 You are now going to work in a project group to analyse a local environmental issue and suggest solutions.

Start by conducting secondary research into your own local area to find out more about:

- your local environment as a place of recreation
- the different **stakeholders** and their activities
- the problem with your local **amenity**
- the causes and consequences of the problem.

You will need to find local sources – articles, blogs, websites, leaflets – that present the issue in a credible and reliable way.

7 Then consider:

- where you can find information to relate these problems to global issues raised by changing environments, growing populations, litter and conservation
- how you can raise awareness of local environmental problems
- what needs to be done to convince people to change their attitudes or behaviour.

8 Finally, use your findings to design and produce a poster or set of slides to raise awareness and persuade others to take the problem seriously. Remember to:

- include secondary research evidence
- use both local and global research to back up your persuasive arguments.

> **❓ REFLECTION POINT**
> - How did you structure your argument to present points memorably and concisely?
> - In what ways did you convince your audience through analysis of facts and statistics?
> - How effective were these methods in raising awareness that the issue you identified is serious?

Vocabulary

stakeholder: any person with an interest or concern in something

amenity: something that provides comfort or enjoyment such as a place to relax and play

Study skills

You may wish to refer to the definition of secondary research from Unit 2.3 and revisit what you learned about causes and consequences in Unit 4.3.

Applying what you have learned: conducting primary research

Skills focus
✓ Research
✓ Analysis
Learning focus
• Select relevant information and arguments.
• Conduct research to support your actions.
• Use primary and secondary research to justify your goal.

Your task

You will work in a group to identify a local action that will improve a local amenity for everyone. You will come up with a goal and an action plan. You will then create a survey to be completed by local users. You will collate and display the results of your research.

Approaching the task

In the previous unit, your group identified a local problem and related it to global issues around conservation, water, climate change or development. In this unit, you are going to work together on a solution.

1 **a)** In your group, identify an action that would help the conservation issue that you identified in your own local area.

b) Consider what kind of local action might make your local environment a better place for everyone.

2 From this action, develop a goal that is SMART: Specific, Measurable, Achievable, Relevant and has a Timeframe.

When coming up with a SMART objective, you will need to:

• Define your goal (**S**pecific)

• Base it on research (**M**easurable)

• Work out who would pay for it or support it (**A**chievable)

• Relate it to global conservation aims (**R**elevant)

• Work out how long it would take (**T**ime frame).

If you completed the Global Perspectives Primary Checkpoint, you will have learned that you need to identify a goal and manage a project that acts towards achieving that goal.

You have now developed a goal that is intended to help solve an issue in your local environment, which is also linked to a global environmental problem.

3 Now you have a timeframe for your goal, as a group complete a planning grid like the one below. In this case, the goal is to rewild the green space behind the school.

Time	Action	Who will do it?	How will you report it?
Week 1	Doing research into biodiversity Obtaining permission from school	Daksha and Lucy Chandice and Farhana	PowerPoint slides about benefits of rewilding Talk to Headteacher or Principal and obtain written permission
Week 2	Digging the plot Planting seeds Putting up notices	All of us	
Week 3	Present what we have done in assembly and why	Anand and Lucy will write scripts; Arun and Frahan will edit slides	We will all present in our section assembly

In Global Perspectives Lower Secondary, you are expected to conduct more research to support your ideas, to analyse the evidence and evaluate what the evidence shows you.

You will need to use the facts and evidence from the previous unit to support your action and prove that it is necessary. Remember that you need to convince and persuade others who may not like change. You will need to:

- find information from reliable sources that presents the global problem
- present different **perspectives** on the local problem
- analyse how conservation projects can help to improve local problems
- suggest what is achievable within your local environment.

For your project to succeed, you need to persuade the stakeholders involved that the action you propose will make their environment better for them.

People can be persuaded more easily if they feel **consulted** and involved. One way to do this is to conduct a **poll** or **survey** and to present the results to show that you have researched and listened to local people's opinions.

> **Vocabulary**
>
> **consult**: to seek information or advice from

> 🔑 **Key terms**
>
> **perspective**: a viewpoint on an issue based on evidence and reasoning
>
> **poll**: asking a set of people to vote on a set of options
>
> **survey**: a set of questions you ask people to gather information or find out their opinions

4. As a group, create a survey to be completed by users of your local amenity. You will need to consider:

   - What are the priorities of the users?

   - How would they like to see the local amenity improve?

   There are many ways of conducting a survey, whether in person or online. Consider:

   - Which would be most time effective for you?

   - How will you find a **sample** of relevant users or stakeholders?

   - How reliable will your information be?

   Discuss your ideas in your group.

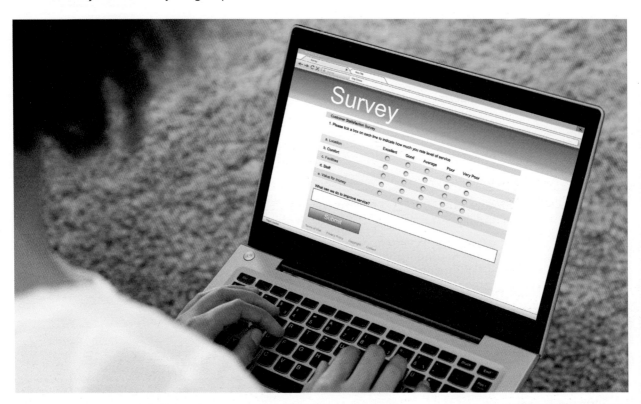

Analysts talk about quantitative and qualitative data, so you will need to make sure your survey can provide:

☐ facts to support your project

☐ opinions that show the need for action.

5. Now you have completed your survey, you need to think about who to send your survey to. Start with people you know and then consider other users that you can easily contact.

   Work out the best means to contact them and the best way to create your survey.

   Read through the 'Checklist for success' on the next page to help you.

Study skills

You can remind yourself of quantitative and qualitative research by revisiting Chapter 2.3. To revisit use of data and predictions, turn to Chapter 3.

Checklist for success

✔ Survey people within your own class and contacts such as parents, teachers and friends.

✔ You could use an online tool in order to ask specific questions in a poll.

✔ Ask a series of questions testing participants' awareness of:

   a) the local conservation issue

   b) their understanding of global conservation issues

   c) whether they agree with your solution for the local problem

   d) ideas about who could pay for it.

✔ Include a range of closed quantitative questions (Yes/No; scale of 1–5) and open qualitative questions ('What do you think…?', 'What else would you like to see…?').

6 Once you have the results from your survey, you'll need to explore them. If you have framed the questions correctly, they should provide information and personal opinions that support your proposed action.

You will need to:

a) extract the data

b) discuss and decide what graphical forms would most usefully present your findings – for example, a bar graph or pie chart

c) use quotations from those you surveyed to support

d) turn the data and opinions into a series of slides, posters or **infographics** – you will use these in the next unit.

Key terms

infographic: chart, illustration or diagram that presents information visually

Reflecting on your progress

- Which questions produced the most useful data?

- How could your group use the opinions that people have expressed?

- Was your sample large enough and representative of the different stakeholders of the local amenity. Did it cover a range of perspectives?

- Do you have enough evidence to show that people would support your action?

- Looking back, how would you have improved your poll to provide better data?

Applying what you have learned: presenting your goal

Your task

You will work together as a group to decide how to present your action plan for a local conservation project, your research findings and your supporting arguments to the rest of the class. You will then create, practise and give your presentation.

Approaching the task

You have proposed an action that will help you to meet local and global goals. You have researched evidence online that will support the need for action, you have a timeframe for action, and you have surveyed stakeholders and found out whether they agree with you. So, what next?

In the real world, you would have a public meeting with a presentation to explain what you propose and to persuade people to support your ideas. You can simulate this in the classroom by presenting your ideas, your research and your findings to the rest of the class.

You will now plan how to present your findings to the rest of the class.

Study skills

Look back at what you have learned about making a presentation in Chapter 5 and teamwork skills in Chapters 5 and 6.

Checklist for success

✔ Include a striking visual opening.

✔ Provide a clear summary of the facts and information.

✔ Give a reasoned argument for your achievable action or goal.

✔ Give supporting evidence, perspectives and reasoning.

✔ Make links between global and local issues.

✔ Include research that shows your action could make a difference.

✔ Present a SMART set of actions that can achieve your goal.

✔ Give evidence of how your action is supported by the poll you conducted and what people have said (quantitative and qualitative research).

✔ Explain how the opinions of those you surveyed support your action.

✔ Use visuals to support your argument.

✔ Have a good balance of pictures, facts and quotations.

✔ Keep the visuals, including slides, short and to the point: the persuasion comes from the way you talk about them.

1 Now decide in your group who is going to do what. You will need to divide the organisation of the presentation between different group members, and then divide up the slides, posters and visuals so that each of you has a slide or sequence of slides to present.

Use the 'Checklist for success' to divide different parts of the presentation between you. Then rehearse your presentation as a group.

2 Make your presentation to the class. You will need to divide up the presentation fairly.

Speak clearly and directly to your audience and do not read from your notes; instead, use notes or slides as prompts for your own persuasive arguments.

Reflecting on your progress

• Which presentation had the clearest goal?

• Which arguments were the most persuasive?

• Which actions sounded most relevant and achievable?

• What skills of persuasion did the group members display?

Reflecting on what you have learned

Your task

You will write an individual personal reflection of up to 500 words on what you have learned from the group task in this chapter.

Approaching the task

At the end of Global Perspectives Primary Checkpoint, you may have added a personal reflection to the team report on what you did. You should have learned that while in Global Perspectives you often work in teams, you learn as individuals.

The purpose of this chapter has been to develop your research, evaluation and communication skills as learners within a team. However, your reflection is personal to you; it is what you see when you look in the mirror.

How can you change what you see in the mirror? In Global Perspectives, there are two types of reflection:

• Reflecting on your thoughts and actions in response to an issue

• Reflecting on the skills you have demonstrated.

Study skills

Reflection is thinking about what you do and how you do it in a way that helps you make progress.

1 a) Look back at your Global Perspectives studies this year: which topic has changed the way you think and act?

b) Which skill do you think you have advanced in the most?

c) How would you demonstrate that you have advanced in this skill?

Discuss your responses with a partner, then share your ideas with the class.

Good reflection needs to be supported by specific examples. You need to link the examples to action or learning that you have done.

2 Working on your own, think about the key turning points in your understanding of an issue you have looked at in Global Perspectives this year.

   a) Give a specific example of learning something new.

   b) Give a specific example of how your past thoughts or actions are different from what you want to do in the future.

Write down your thoughts and reflections.

3 Reflect on your skills development throughout this year's course.

   a) How many skills are there in Global Perspectives? Choose *two* of those skills.

   b) How has your understanding of *each* of these two skills developed in the last year? Give specific examples that prove this.

   c) How do the examples prove your points about skills development?

Discuss your responses with a partner, then feed back to the class.

4 Write a personal reflection on what you have learned from the group task in this chapter. You can write up to 500 words.

To structure your reflection, consider:

   a) How has your understanding of conservation developed?

   b) Has this changed how you think or act?

   c) How much did you contribute to your team's ideas, action and presentation?

   d) Did your team work well?

   e) Which of the six Global Perspectives skills are your strengths? Which are your areas for development?

Reflecting on your progress

Reflection needs an organised structure.

* How have your thoughts about what reflection means developed and changed?

* How has your behaviour or the behaviour of other people changed as a result of what you have learned or done?

* What is the link between those changes and what you have discovered or done?

* Have you balanced out your own individual strengths and weaknesses in your learning and activities?

Check your progress

Beginning	Developing	Going beyond
• I can identify news articles and websites giving different perspectives on an issue.	• I can recognise bias and identify the purpose of news articles and websites.	• I can evaluate the reliability and credibility of news articles and websites.
• I can consider arguments and explore how convincing they are.	• I can evaluate arguments and recognise their strengths and weaknesses.	• I can evaluate how persuasive an argument is in terms of its structure and use of evidence.
• I can present information and opinions and recognise which is which.	• I can present information and opinions to support my own reasoning.	• I can present information and opinions referencing sources (both global and local) to support my reasoning.
• I can identify the skills I have practised in an activity and my strengths and weaknesses.	• I can reflect on my skills and those of my team in carrying out an activity, identifying and balancing out strengths and weaknesses.	• I can evaluate how I have developed my skills and identify targets for improvement, relating them directly to what I have learned during an activity.

Next steps

- Explore other conservation issues in your local area. What actions would make a difference? Are these actions you can carry out yourself or encourage others to do?

- Think about how you can develop the Global Perspectives skill that you have identified as a weakness. What would help: more reading, more internet research or more work with others? Which other curriculum subjects could you use to improve that skill?

Glossary of key terms

abbreviations: shortened versions of words or phrases.

annotating: adding notes to text or a diagram to explain or comment on its features.

argument: a series of statements containing reasons and evidence which support a claim about a global issue.

assertion: a claim made without supporting evidence.

axis: a line on a graph showing a scale of measurement.

bias: favouring one person or point of view over another in a way considered to be unfair.

cartogram: some maps use colours or shading or icons to show data; a cartogram changes the size and shape of countries to do this.

cause: something that makes something else happen; the reason why something happened.

collaboration: working together with others to produce or achieve something.

communicating: exchanging information with others.

consequence: the effect or effects something has; what happened because of something: something that makes something else happen; the reason why something happened.

correlation: relationship or connection between two or more factors, for example heart rate and life expectancy.

deadline: a set time or date by which you must complete a task.

ethos: aims and values.

evaluate: make a judgement about something's worth or effectiveness.

evidence: information about a global issue that helps to develop understanding or prove that something is true or false.

feedback: information given about the results of an activity that is intended to improve results next time the activity is done.

generalising: making a general rule or statement that is then applied to other cases.

globalisation: when what was local and national becomes global because of increasing connections around the world. For example, pizza was once local (Naples, Italy) and is now global.

graphical: information given in the form of a graph.

infographic: chart, illustration or diagram that presents information visually.

interpretation: an explanation or opinion as to why something is a certain way.

interview: a conversation in which one person asks another person questions.

in the field: a particular location (such as a market) where research is carried out.

issue: an important subject or problem for discussion.

multiple-choice: a question with a limited set of answers, for example 'What time did you arrive? a) 9:00 a.m. b) 11:00 a.m. c) 1:00 p.m.'

non-verbal gestures: movements you make such as pointing or shrugging your shoulders.

numerical: information given in the form of numbers.

open question: a question that requires an explanation or longer answer, for example 'How did you feel when…?'

per capita: the total amount of something in a country divided by the number of people in the country.

perspective: a viewpoint on an issue based on evidence and reasoning.

pitch: how high or low your voice sounds.

poll: asking a set of people to vote on a set of opinions or an issue.

prediction: a statement about what will happen in the future.

primary research: research you do yourself, for example interviewing people.

qualitative research: where the answers tell you how people or groups of people feel or what they think.

quantitative research: where the answers can be measured and compared in the form of numbers.

questionnaire: a written set of questions requiring a response.

rate: the change of one quantity compared to another, for example the change in life expectancy over time in years.

reflection: thinking carefully about what you do or have done (and how you do it) in a way that helps you make progress.

research: investigating an issue or topic to find out more about it.

sample: (when carrying out a survey) a group of people chosen out of a larger number in order to get information about the larger group; representative samples should try to include the types of people within the larger group.

scan: to run your eyes over a text looking for particular information or words and phrases.

secondary research: research done using other people's research findings.

single-use plastic: products made from plastic that are designed to be used just once and then thrown away.

source: a reference text or other form of information.

stakeholder: someone with a specific interest or involvement in something.

survey: to ask a series of questions to find out information about a particular subject or to find out different people's opinions.

take turns: where one person speaks first, then another, and so on.

trend: the general movement or direction of development over time.

valid: based in truth; supported by evidence.

Acknowledgements

Text and figures

We are grateful to the following for permission to reproduce copyright material. In some instances, we have been unable to trace the owners of copyright material, and we would appreciate any information that would enable us to do so.

An extract on p.16 from www.schoolsforthefuture.co.uk. Reproduced with permission of Schools for the Future, Central Bedfordshire Council; An extract on p.16 from www.typekids.com>blog>schools-of-the-future. Reproduced with permission of TypeKids; Extracts on pp.16, 18 from World Economic Forum: 'Schools of the Future', 2020, Green School International, https://www.greenschool.org/insights/world-economic-forum-schools-of-the-future-2020/, copyright © World Economic Forum, 2022; An extract on p.22 from 'Revitalising the River Ver', St Albans City & District Council, 02/09/2021, https://www.stalbans.gov.uk/revitalising-river-ver. Reproduced with permission; An extract on p.24 from 'Freshwater ecosystems'. Source: Conservation International, https://www.conservation.org/priorities/fresh-water. Reproduced with permission; An extract on p.25 from 'Our River: The River Ver and its People', Ver Valley Society, https://www.riverver.co.uk/our-river/. Reproduced with kind permission; An extract on p.26 from 'Education Study Finds in Favour of Traditional Teaching Styles' by Richard Adams, *The Guardian*, 31/10/2014, copyright © Guardian News & Media Ltd, 2022; Plan on p.32 of Chaoyang Future School, Beijing, Architect: Crossboundaries, plan graphic by Crossboundaries. Reproduced with permission; Figures 3.2.1–3.2.3 on pp.40, 42, 43 maps drawn by Collins Bartholomew adapted from the source data in 'Life expectancy in 1800, 1950 and 2015' in *Life Expectancy* by Max Roser, Esteban Ortiz-Ospina and Hannah Ritchie, Our World in Data. Based on Riley (2006), Gapminder, United Nations Population Division. Licensed under CC-BY-SA by Max Roser, http://ourworldindata.org/life-expectancy. First published in 2013; last revised in October 2019; Figure 3.5.1, p.52 'Life expectancy at birth, 1970 and 2019 (or nearest year)' *Health at a Glance* 2021: OECD Indicators, OECD Publishing, Paris, 2021, https://doi.org/10.1787/ae3016b9-en. Permission conveyed through the Copyright Clearance Center; Figure 4.2.2, p.65 map drawn by Collins Bartholomew based on data from 'McDonald's Restaurants', No. 1070 https://worldmapper.org/maps/foodchains-mcdonalds-2018, copyright © WorldMapper, 2022; An extract on p.70 from 'Food production emissions make up more than a third of global total' by Krista Charles, New Scientist, 13/09/2021, copyright © *New Scientist* Ltd, 2021. Distributed by Tribune Content Agency. All rights reserved; Extracts on p.92 from 'Eleanor Roosevelt: My Day Index' https://erpapers.columbian.gwu.edu/my-day-index. Reproduced with permission of Olswanger Literary LLC; Diagram on p.93 'The Simplest Experiential Learning Cycle' compiled by Andrea Corney, adapted from https://www.edbatista.com/2007/10/experiential.html, Oct 21, 2007. Reproduced by permission of Ed Batista, Executive Coaching; An extract on p.113 adapted from '6 world of work trends set to shape 2022', World Economic Forum, https://www.weforum.org/agenda/2022/01/6-world-of-work-trends-that-will-shape-2022/, 07/01/2022, copyright © World Economic Forum, 2022; and an extract on pp.120–121 from 'Floods and mud: what's happening with Verulamium Lake?' by Laura Bill, *The Herts Advertiser*, 02/09/2021. Reproduced with permission.

Images

We are grateful for the following for permission to reproduce their images:

Cover: underdog_cg/Shutterstock, p.1 ESB Professional/Shutterstock, p.2 J Marshall – Tribaleye Images/Alamy Photographer: NASA/digitaleye, p.3 Manu M Mair/Shutterstock, p.4 akiyoko/Shutterstock, p.4 milatas/Shutterstock, p.4 YSK1/Shutterstock, p.6 Bear Fotos/Shutterstock, p.6 De Visu/Shutterstock, p.6 Prostock-studio/Shutterstock, p.6 Constantine Pankin/Shutterstock, p.9 josepmarti/Shutterstock, p.11 Rudmer Zwerver/Shutterstock, p.12 Tom Wang/Shutterstock, p.12 Rawpixel.com/Shutterstock, p.13 Richard Juilliart/Shutterstock, p.14 CRS PHOTO/Shutterstock, p.15 yogendrasingh.in/Shutterstock, p.17 Egoitz Bengoetxea/Shutterstock, p.18 Paul Prescott/Shutterstock, p.19. Chaoyang Future School, Beijing, Architect: Crossboundaries, Photo by WANG Ziling, p.20 Antonio Guillem/Shutterstock, p.21 Odua Images/Shutterstock, p.22 Paul Prescott/Shutterstock, p.24 Backgroundy/Shutterstock, p.25 Just dance/Shutterstock, p.27 Juice Verve/Shutterstock, p.28 Prostock-studio/Shutterstock, p.29 Odua Images/Shutterstock, p.31 insta_photos/Shutterstock, p.33 AnnaStills/Shutterstock, p.35 sirtravelalot/Shutterstock, p.36 Tewan Banditrakkanka/Shutterstock, p.36 Bangkoker/Shutterstock, p.37 Maria Spb/Shutterstock, p.37 Four Oaks/Shutterstock, p.37 Neirfy/Shutterstock, p.37 Ammit Jack/Shutterstock, p.44 Drop of Light/Shutterstock, p.44 Diego Cervo/Shutterstock, p.47 Zurijeta/Shutterstock, p.48 Kordin Viacheslav/Shutterstock, p.49 Sathit/Shutterstock, p.49 Top Photo Engineer/Shutterstock, p.49 sirtravelalot/Shutterstock, p.50 Ikebana Art-studio/Shutterstock, p.50 ThanakritR/Shutterstock, p.52 Dan Negureanu/Shutterstock, p.53 Gustavo Frazao/Shutterstock, p.54 stockfour/Shutterstock, p.56 Atstock Productions/Shutterstock, p.59 Nikola Bilic/Shutterstock, p.60 Yeti studio/Shutterstock, p.60 ShotPrime Studio/Shutterstock, p.61 based on image by aelitta/Shutterstock, p.62 illpaxphotomatic/Shutterstock, p.63 Chatham172/Shutterstock, p.67 Darryl Brooks/Shutterstock, p.68 ZouZou/Shutterstock, p.69 anarociogf/Shutterstock, p.70 Julia Merska/Shutterstock, p.70 Anastasia_Panait/Shutterstock, p.70 Rich Carey/Shutterstock, p.70 Aleksandar Mijatovic/Shutterstock, p.70 Victor De Schwanberg/Science Photo Library/Alamy Stock Photo, p.71 SherSor/Shutterstock, p.71 bonchan/Shutterstock, p.72 AJP/Shutterstock, p.73 Dokshin Vlad/Shutterstock, p.73 s_bukley/Shutterstock, p.73 DFree/Shutterstock, p.75 mapsandphotos/Shutterstock, p.75 mapsandphotos/Shutterstock, p.75 mapsandphotos/Shutterstock, p.75 Mint Fox/Shutterstock, p.79 Markus Pfaff/Shutterstock, pp.80– 81 Everett Collection Historical/Alamy Stock Photo, p.81 Everett Collection Historical/Alamy Stock Photo, p.82 Krakenimages.com/Shutterstock, p.82 fizkes/Shutterstock, p.83 Fast Speeds Imagery/Shutterstock, p.83 Daisy Daisy/Shutterstock, p.84 illustration by Jouve UK © HarperCollins Publishers 2022, p.85 illustration by Jouve UK © HarperCollins Publishers 2022, p.86 fizkes/Shutterstock, p.87 ARegina/Shutterstock, p.88 Reuters/Alamy Stock Photo, p.90 Rido/Shutterstock, p.91 AnnaStills/Shutterstock, p.92 Cvandyke/Shutterstock, p.93 Bangkok Click Studio/Shutterstock, p.94 UN Photo/Greg Kinch, p.96 DrAndY/Shutterstock, p.97 milatas/Shutterstock, p.99 Gorodenkoff/Shutterstock, p.100 Alamy Stock Photo (ES Royalty Free), p.101 Fotokostic/Shutterstock, p.102 MBI/Alamy Stock Photo Photographer: Stockbroker, p.103 smolaw/Shutterstock, p.104 Rawpixel.com/Shutterstock, p.105 Juice Flair/Shutterstock, p.106 Michael Gordon/Shutterstock, p.107 Rawpixel.com/Shutterstock, p.108 Atstock Productions/Shutterstock, p.109 Cavan-Images/Shutterstock, p.110 soft_light/Shutterstock, p.113 Smile Fight/Shutterstock, p.113 David Prado Perucha/Shutterstock, p.113 SofikoS/Shutterstock, p.115 PradeepGaurs/Shutterstock, p.116 Rido/Shutterstock, p.116 littleWhale/Shutterstock, p.119 Julian Nieman/Alamy Stock Photo, p.120 Aaron Jacob copyright © Aaron Jacob, p.122 PCJones/Alamy Stock Photo, p.123 SeraphP/Shutterstock, p.124 Elena Berd/Shutterstock, p.126 CRS PHOTO/Shutterstock, p.127 JoshoJosho/Shutterstock, p.128 encierro/Shutterstock, p.128 PRASANNAPIX/Shutterstock, p.129 BearFotos/Shutterstock, p.130 Andrey_Popov/Shutterstock, p.131 marut BaBa/Shutterstock, p.132 Rawpixel.com/Shutterstock, p.134 True Touch Lifestyle/Shutterstock, p.135 carballo/Shutterstock.